I0830042

Reviews

Five Million Steps is a winner. You do not have to be a hiker to enjoy the kind of adventurous life found on the Appalachian Trail. It is a life most of us will never be able to enjoy except through the eyes, ears, heart, and pen of people like Lon Chenowith. You will be richly rewarded by getting to know the heart and story of this humble, sensitive, and rugged outdoorsman. He carved enough time out of fourteen years to hike over two thousand miles of demanding climbs and terrain while carrying some 30-40 pounds to complete what few have ever done. There is something about this kind of life that draws men to abandon the safe and the easy. Although I never physically took one step alongside him on this incredible journey, I have experienced his joy in the unpredictable, majestic, beautiful, God-glorifying creation we so often take for granted. I invite you to take the journey for yourself. Of course, anyone so bold as to be planning to hike the two-thousand-mile trail will find a true traveling companion in *Five Million Steps*.

--Richard Emmert (1944-2015), Morristown, Tennessee

Five Million Steps is much more than a day-to-day journal of the adventure of hiking the Appalachian Trail. Stories of events and thoughts give insight to the faith and the character of the author written to capture the reader's interest.

--Ross "Mississippi" Sherman, Wiggins, Mississippi

It is funny how the mind works. Of the 276 miles I hiked with my true friend and accomplished outdoorsman, I can only recall wonderful memories of the mountains climbed, meals and burdens shared, prayers, laughs, and even sore and tired bodies. *Arkansas Traveler*'s detailed retelling of his trek is a joy to read and a help for any aspiring distance hiker. I hope you enjoy it as much as I have.

--Eric "Prune Picker" Greer, Perris, California

Lon has captured the many emotions of hiking the AT, from despair to sheer joy, from body aches to soaring spirits. He shares the tedium of hiking day after day in the rain to the real joy of the trail, and the people you will meet both on and off the trail. The injection of his original poetry simply adds more depth to this story of a multiple-year odyssey to travel the spine of the Appalachian Mountains.

--Ken "Gray Panter" Stone, Williston, Vermont

Many individuals dream of exciting adventures, but for most the dream never progresses beyond the talking stage. My good friend, Lon Chenowith, jumps in with both feet, rain or shine, snow or heat. In completing the Appalachian Trail as a section-hiker, he shows readers a dream can be accomplished in stages. He has inspired me to a similar kind of adventure—a bicycle ride the length of my home state of Tennessee. Lon's account of his adventure gives you a feel of the beauty, the challenge, the joys, and the frustrations of hiking the famous Appalachian Trail.

--Bill Horner, Caryville, Tennessee

As one who has hiked and mountain biked with Lon in the wilderness, I can say that Lon is physically and mentally tough, determined to finish the trail; and at the same time, passionate about the beauty of God's nature. A must read for anyone curious about the physical, emotional, and spiritual hardships of the AT. [You will] experience Lon's nuggets and pearls of wisdom along the path to the mountain top.

--Mark Weiler, Greeley, Colorado

As a fellow Appalachian Trail section-hiker, this book inspires me to get out and not to give up on my dream to someday complete the journey. If you're a hiker or any sort of adventurer, this will be a book that will be hard to put down.

--John "Morning Glory" Jordan, Johnson City, Tennessee

FIVE MILLION STEPS

Faith Adventures along the Appalachian Trail

Second Edition

Lon Chenowith

Dedication

This book is dedicated to the One who so seldom gets the credit for the grace in every day, the wonders of creation, and the care in every mile we travel. His glory is seen even when it rains, in the breaking snowdrifts on the mountainside, in the slick and slide of mud up to the ankles, and the worst of conditions in the wilderness.

Hiking the Appalachian Trail has done much to deepen my awe of the gifts of heaven tucked into every day. If earth is so full of undiscovered majesties, just think of the rapture in heaven! If the trail was so replete with colorful personalities—just think of walking with godly characters from the ages.

Acknowledgements

I will lift up my eyes unto the hills, from whence cometh my help. My help cometh from the Lord, which made heaven and earth. He will not suffer thy foot to be moved: He that keepeth thee will not slumber...The Lord shall preserve thy going out and thy coming in from this time forth, even forevermore. **(Psalm 121:1-3, 8)**

I humbly acknowledge my sweetheart Kay, who prayed as I took those five million steps, our children, who grew up with the saga of each mountain trek and tolerated my absences. They share a love for the outdoors to this day. Our sons backpack in many places around the world and our daughter loves to hike.

My family's vacations were sacrificed for this dream of mine. Initially, it was family time—Dad's idea of vacation. For the last ten years it was just Dad alone in the wilderness. They had much patience and forbearance in my long trek north.

Likewise, I acknowledge my parents, Bill (1933-2016) and Madeline Cooper, who have always encouraged me to climb a little higher, and my sweetheart's parents, Dr. Joseph (1915-2007) and Eva Shelley (1920-2019), who over time grew to accept my crazy adventures. They were and are my heroes in this life. What a gift from above they were to my family.

My mother-in-law once wrote this ditty about my mountain travels:

He says he's part Indian,
we think it's true.
He likes the mountain trail,
just like they do.
He could live in a tent
the rest of his life.
If only he had married
a "young" Indian wife!

During the entire fourteen-year section hike along the Appalachian Trail, I was the pastor of a few hundred people in a small mountain town in East Tennessee. Many of the people there cheered me on and looked forward to the trail stories upon my return.

Special thanks to my hiking partner, *Prune Picker* (Eric Greer), who hiked 276 miles on the Appalachian Trail. We were seminary brothers back in the mid-80's and friends ever since. He has been an inspiration and the only partner who every came back to hike again.

Heartfelt thanks to *Gray Panter* (Ken Stone)—who you will meet from the great state of Vermont. Both *Gray Panter* and *Prune Picker* provided many of the photos found here. They captured just a little of the majesty the Appalachians have for any outdoor enthusiast who shares a love for the wilderness.

Special acknowledgement to *Mississippi* (Ross Sherman) who provided encouragement and helped me access the trail in Virginia where he served as a volunteer in the forest service after a distinguished career protecting the woodlands in his home state.

Many thanks to those who have proofed, corrected, and assisted in the repeated drafts of this manuscript. Humble thanks to Mary Reynolds for her patience and perseverance in formatting this second edition.

Close to a thousand copies went out for the first edition. This second edition comes more than ten years later. The second edition gets *Five Million Steps* back in circulation for those who have requested copies.

Lon Chenowith
Forest City, North Carolina
First Edition: May 2009
Second Edition: October 2020

TABLE OF CONTENTS

FOREWORD

On my desk at home lies a small granite rock. Under it is a laminated poem by my dear friend, Lon, the *Arkansas Traveler*. It reads:

The Katahdin Rock

Pursue your dreams.
No matter how long.
No matter how hard.
No matter how high.
Come to the image of God.

I love that poem and many others Lon wrote in this wonderful book. You must know as you read this book that Lon is a very unusual, uncommon man. He is a rugged outdoorsman, poet, storyteller, staunchly loyal friend, and a man after God's heart. I know this because we have spent time together—on the trail.

But it is his attention to detail that makes this book so valuable. Where so many others generalize their experiences and advice, Lon records for you from his notes on the trail invaluable lessons, encounters, stories, tips, and images which will help you succeed in hiking and life.

It was such a pleasure being his hiking partner on several sections of the Appalachian Trail. We laughed a lot, prayed together, and talked like men seldom do. He taught me that it is not muscle but will that keep a hiker going. And I learned to appreciate the comedy that occurs when, as he puts it, backpacking romance meets backcountry reality.

If you are considering tackling the Appalachian Trail, this book will be of immense help. If you hiked the trail in recent years, chances are you will find your name and story inside these pages or remember your encounter with the *Arkansas Traveler*.

I hope you enjoy reading this book as much as I have. And when you are finished, hit the trail.

--Prune Picker

INTRODUCTION: THE CALL OF THE WILD

Man cannot tell this side of heaven why he is made like he is made. I have always had an affinity for the woodlands and the wild places. Since my teen years, I have read about the Appalachian Trail and dreamed about walking all the way to Maine.

My wife wishes I had hiked it in college years, but work and school kept me busy. Those college days did provide great memories backpacking the Ouachita Mountains in Oklahoma, Big Bend National Park in southwest Texas, and Organ Pipe Cactus National Monument just outside of Ajo, Arizona.

In seminary I met my sweetheart, who loves a good seven-mile hike, but not seventeen in one stretch. We started a new church in the Everglades and rebuilt a fallen church in the Mid-Ohio Valley of West Virginia, and then we moved our family to East Tennessee. That is when the call of the wild became undeniable.

Springer Mountain was fairly close, so I reached for that seventeen-year-old dream. It has been some kind of adventure for a family man with twenty-one days off a year. The logistics were more challenging than the terrain, the climbs, and the twenty-mile days.

I made very little progress those first few years. By the time I hit the Virginia highlands, I knew if I didn't step it up, it would be a twenty-year project. Those mountain miles have been an annual highlight without a doubt, but the people were the best part of the journey.

These are the stories of a northbound section-hiker, traveling for over a decade on top of the eastern highlands of America. It seemed like I chewed up more hiking partners than miles the first few years until I learned that the way to make the miles was in solitude.

In those Georgia ridges my trail name became *Arkansas Traveler*, derived from my native state and its folklore, and a love for travel far and wide. Honestly, there were times I would ask myself, "Why am I doing this again?" It didn't take too many miles to find the answer. The call of the wild was this backpacker's way of saying there was an itch for the wilderness, where life was reduced to simple things—kind acts, nature's glories, and overcoming the odds that were sure to come.

It is a calling away from desks and offices to a climb above town life and beyond alarm clocks. The deluge of news and information was scarce out there, where life was defined by real conversation, a Lipton noodle meal, checks on water supply, early bunk time, and doctoring the feet for another day of mountain climbing.

It took a certain kind of makeup to be able to keep going, and for some, to keep coming back. You cannot allow thirst, raw blisters, rocks galore, a straight climb up, hard down hills, creek crossings, or over-friendly mice to distract you. After all, when you add up all the miles and the mountains, it is a journey of five million steps. It is a long passage that thousands have started every year, but only a few hundred actually finish.

The worst part of the trail for me was the downpours that cut visibility under a poncho and zapped the joy right out of the adventure. But there were times I was so glad to be out there—even when the trail became awash, I could climb on with glee. In less dignified times, I would shout in despair until I felt ashamed.

Out of the euphoria and the drudgery there were remarkable accounts from the unpredictable nature of gripping the trekking poles and looking north. Here are the stories of adventure, faith, and the intrigue just as they were while walking in the heart of America's greatest wild lands.

Arkansas Traveler and *Prune Picker* overlooking the rolling farm land of Pennsylvania. Altogether Prune Picker hiked 276 miles on the AppalachianTrail through Virginia, Pennsylvania, Connecticut, Massachusetts, and Vermont.

Which by strength setteth fast the mountains; being girded with power. (Psalm 65:6)

Backpacking the Appalachian Trail

Year	Days	Trips	Trail Miles	Destination
1994	1-5	1	50.7	Unicoi Gap, GA
1995	6-10	2	53.0	Wallace Gap, NC
1996	11-16	3	59.8	Fontana Dam, NC
1997	17-19	2	21.2	Russell Field, TN
1998	20-28	4	129.7	Sam's Gap, NC
1999	29-40	1	189.0	Dickey Gap, VA
2000	41-48	2	145.2	Salt Sulfur, VA
2001	49-53	1	67.7	Daleville, VA
2002	54-70	2	274.5	Bear Den Rocks, VA
2003	71-87	2	254.1	Palmerton, PA
2004	88-110	2	353.4	Bennington, VT
2005	111-125	2	232.6	Crawford Notch, NH
2006	126-134	1	88.1	Andover, ME
2007	135-149	1	256.5	Mount Katahdin, ME
14 Years	149	26	2,172.8 miles	14 States

Map of the Appalachian Trail

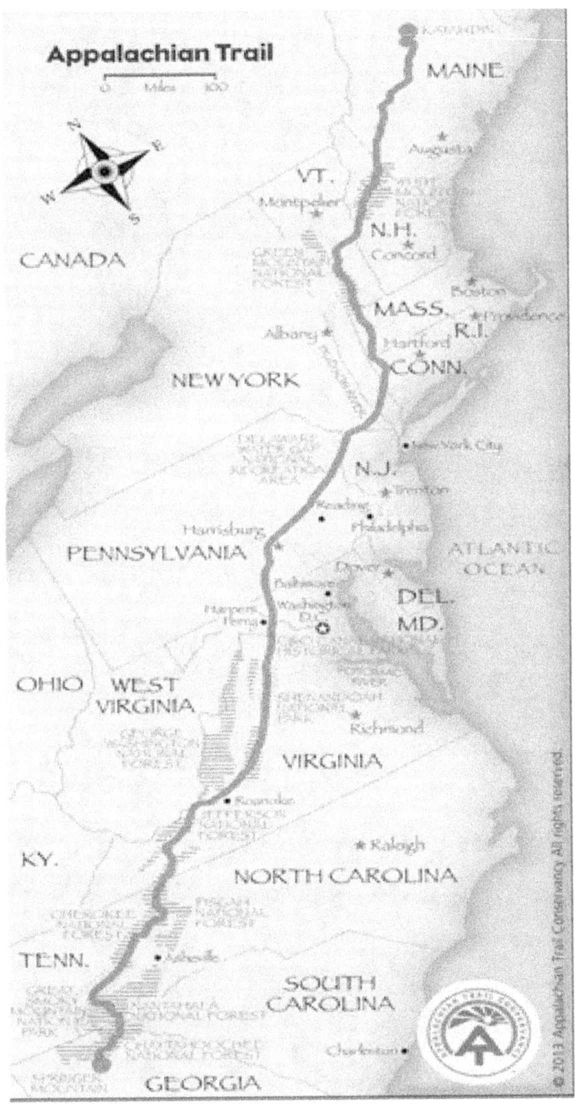

Used by permission from the
Appalachian Trail Conservancy

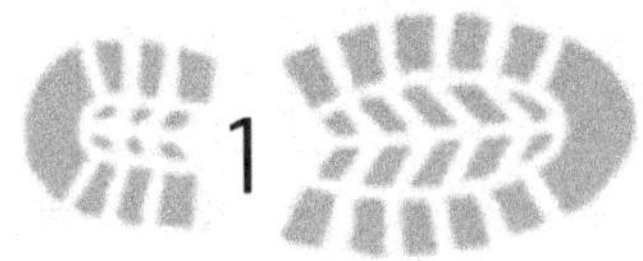

THE *ARKANSAS TRAVELER*

Almost all long-distance hikers choose a trail name for themselves, or another hiker tags them with one along the first few miles of the trek.

One of the most memorable pairs I met through the years was *Crash* and *Burn*. They were two young ladies who started out with a young man who planned to hike all 2,170 miles. He had pulled out after a few hundred miles and they kept going. They were both under the age of twenty, one from Virginia and the other from Tennessee.

They gave each other their monikers. One was named *Crash* because she kept falling, taking a tumble over roots and rocks. *Burn* got her trail name because she had burned supper a time or two.

Others I remember were *Father Time* and *Mother Goose, Cliff Dancer, Backtracker, Teasel* and *DNA Dave, Salamander, Woodchuck, Kat* and *Sparrow, Big Green Hat, Spider, Fly Boy, Lady Leaper,* and *Dolphin,* to name a few.

A Kentucky Park Ranger who dreamed of hiking the trail trained and started her trek in Georgia. The first day out she came into the shelter (placed every 7 miles or so along the white-blazed path in between towns) without a trail name. She was so happy to be out there. She took off her scarf and started dancing next to the trail shelter where she planned to spend the night. She thought she was all alone—but she wasn't. Another hiker gave her the name *Dances with Scarf.*

My trail name hails from my native state. In Arkansas folklore, Colonel Sanford Faulkner (1807-1874) told the story of a traveler on horseback that was lost in the western mountains in the part of the state where my extended family comes from. The stranger was both tired and hungry, as was his horse. He knew night was coming when he spied a cabin owned by a squatter's family. When he trotted up to the porch, the man of the house was playing a tune on his fiddle.

The traveler talked for over half-an-hour and learned absolutely nothing while his nerves were frayed by the fiddle playing, for the squatter played the same tune over and over again. He finally asked the man for some food and water. A humorous exchange between the two men went on for another long spell. The one said he had nothing in the house. The other asked how far the next place might be. The squatter didn't know because he had never been there.

The traveler invited himself for a night's lodging. The fiddler said there was only one dry spot in the house and that was for him and his wife. "Why not fix the roof?" asked the stranger. "Can't fix it on no rainy day," replied the man of the house. All the while the squatter played the same sour notes as dusk began to fall upon the outline of the mountains. Finally, the traveler barked, "Why don't you finish that tune?"

The squatter paused and said he only learned it yesterday, and he was afraid he would forget the first line. The stranger took the fiddle, tuned the strings, and swung right into the second part of the song. The hound on the porch woke up. The squatter danced a jig, and his family came out of the shack.

That night, the traveler had the prime part of the buck killed that morning, corn for his horse, and a swig out of the black jug. What is more, he slept on the dry spot. The year was 1840, and the story of the Arkansas Traveler has been told ever since. There's a song that goes along with the folktale:

On a lonely road quite long ago,
A trav'ler trod with fiddle and bow;
While rambling thru the country rich and grand,
He quickly sensed the magic and the beauty of the land.

Chorus
For the wonder state we'll sing a song,
And lift our voices loud and long.
For the wonder state we'll shout hurrah,
And praise the opportunities we find in Arkansas.

Many years have passed, the trav'lers gay,
Repeat the tune along the highway;
And every voice that sings the glad refrain
Re-echoes from the mountains to the fields of growing grain.

Repeat Chorus

1 Lyrics by the Arkansas State Song Selection Committee, 1947. Music by Colonel Sanford Faulkner, 1850.

A FOOLHARDY START

This is one of those true-life tales of surviving Dad's vacation. My boys were eight and eleven. In June of that first year, when Georgia was boiling, I led those innocent cotton-tops on a 56.5 mile hike in five days from Amicalola Falls to Unicoi Gap.

As a father, I wanted my boys to have a love for the outdoors and share experiences that they would forever remember. My good intentions were never in question, but my wisdom was. Our backpacking adventure was one few men would do, yet I unwittingly enlisted my two young sons to pay the painful price of my dream.

The intent was for father and sons to hike the most famous footpath on earth section-by-section, from Georgia all the way to Maine, bit-by-bit, mile-by-mile. While thru-hikers do the entire two thousand plus mile trail in four to six months, I hoped we could do it as section-hikers over a span of a few years.

The backpacks became heavier the higher we climbed. We made them a little lighter when the food bag was reduced by our hearty appetites. In those summer days, we packed a pair of shorts and a couple of short-sleeved cotton shirts (a year or two later, I gladly traded the cotton for lighter and quick-drying cool max varieties), a medical kit, water and food supplies, and maps. Only my eldest son and I carried packs. We climbed the mountain trail as the sweat soaked us and rolled off our faces in big, salty drops. No, summer in Georgia was not a good time to get started.

This was not a great example of how to have good father and son time. If it had been a little less humid, or if there had been a little more water, and if we had a little more time to explore, it might have been a cherished memory. Unfortunately, it was a nightmare for them. That is how I lost my first hiking partners.

The carrot for such abuse was an Appalachian Trail t-shirt and ball cap—but they had to do the entire fifty plus miles! Talk about cruel and unusual punishment—and we hiked that hard Georgia terrain not at a boy's pace, but at a man's pace.

We should have known something was not right when my wife and daughter drove us to the access point some six miles up to the Nimberwill Gap on United States Forest Service (USFS) Road 28. My wife put in a praise cassette tape and sang herself all the way back down that mountain gravel road, a bit terrified as a city girl.

It would take years to learn to plan better and work the logistics of section-hiking the Appalachian Trail. One thing we learned that first year was to stick to pick-up points on pavement, places that could be found without a detailed county map.

The boys and I hiked the 2.8 miles to the southern terminus of the trail. We took pictures, and I had a dream come true while those poor lads began their nightmare. They were about to undertake what most grown men could not do.

The youngest became the trailblazer, leading the way until his energy crashed. The eldest loved the outdoors and was very much at home in the woods, even in the heat of the summer. Both boys enjoyed much of the trail, just not the sweat, thirst and blisters.

There they are, two lads at the mercy of their father's high adventures. Out of all the partners I had, honestly, they were some of the toughest.

Altogether, that first day out we hiked 13.3 miles, but just 8.1 miles on the Appalachian Trail. We had agreed to meet the girls at USFS 42, not realizing it crossed the trail more than once. We hiked three miles trying to find them.

The last two hours of that afternoon were committed to eating the dust off the gravel road. Buzzy Bennett, a forest service worker and licensed Southern Baptist preacher, picked us up and helped us link up with the girls. We had a town meal and bedded down in the comfort of a motel room that night.

The next four days were a mixture of elation and torture.Gnats chewed on the youngest son. He was especially subject to their pestilence. His skin would swell up in big red welts, adding to his misery. After slapping gnats and a few mosquitoes, enduring the heat, and covering all those Georgia mountain miles, his little face would show such relief when the end of the trail came. He would run out of the woods to greet his mother at the trailhead parking lot, where she would be waiting for us with cold drinks.

Blood Mountain

The boys liked the third day best of all. We climbed Blood Mountain, where the Cherokee and Creek Indians fought until the mountain was red with their blood. There, I reminded the boys they had a little Cherokee blood from a great great-grandmother and great great-grandfather who survived the "Trail of Tears."

The only downside of Blood Mountain was that there were more than one million bees in pursuit of early summer blooms. Four hornets landed on the eight-year-old's pants and canteen. He had always been highly allergic to bee stings. I quickly brushed them away. He was fortunate to escape without a single sting.

The oldest has never forgotten that mountain and the stone shelter perched there. The mountain had a stone surface on top with very little vegetation. We saw deer, woodpecker, a covey of quail, a hornet's nest, and met two Boy Scout troops. Blood Mountain was unlike any other mountain climb in Georgia because it was teeming with wildlife, rich in history, and had some noteworthy views—the kind of views that the boys expected in every mile of the Appalachian Trail.

The last two days we didn't see any other hikers. It was rainy and stormy. We came upon a wounded hawk right on the trail and got off the footpath to give him berth. We spotted a turkey and a snake.

The youngest son didn't make the last day and failed to qualify for his Appalachian Trail t-shirt—what a Dad! The eleven-year-old was a little tougher. He took all the punishment his Dad gave out. So he earned both the hat and the t-shirt.

In the years to come, the boys returned to the trail, but never with the same enthusiasm that I foolishly kicked out of them. We laugh about it today, though I was the one who should have been kicked. They still like to hike, but they prefer just a few miles.

It was a haphazard adventure and one that had more zeal than reason, more idealism than sense. It should have been a trip planned with plenty of time to explore, more camping than conquering the miles, and more treats in the packs than the taste of sweat and tears.

Yes, we succeeded in completing the fifty-plus miles, but in the process, I failed to take the time to get down to their level of development and adventure. I pushed them and I pushed myself, and we were all glad it was over.

Black Bear Encounters

One year and a month later back out on the trail, I subconsciously decided to up the ante on stupidity and stretch those boys of mine just a little further. I led the charge on a sixteen-mile hike, and we started after lunch! It was a logistical disaster. It would be a day to remember—but not the kind you would want to—it would have been best forgotten.

All day long we saw only a solitary lady hiker. We took in a lot of wilderness in quick time and prayed, prayed, prayed. By the time we came out at the trailhead parking lot, there had been a few tears and many miles of regret on my part.

We stumbled onto the highway about 9:30 pm, greeted by the high beams of the Aerostar van with two shadowy figures inside: one worried mother and a curious little sister: "Why is Daddy hiking in the dark?"

Needless to say, we were one less hiker the next day. The youngest decided Mom was sane and safe, Dad, not so much. The oldest son and I finished up Georgia the second day and met only one gentleman hiker. We rolled out the sleeping bags at Muskrat Creek Shelter, and there we finally took a little joy in the camping experience.

During that night, quiet conversation unfolded between my son and I as the lights in the heavens went out and the night sounds filled the dark space outside the shelter. A wiser father would have known that such moments were the point of the journey, not how many miles were conquered.

My sons and I never spoke about whether they enjoyed those grueling hikes. They knew if they went with Dad, they were not to complain—just be tough, stretch out, and get it done. Even so, they let me know when it did meet their expectations. Their eyes danced and their exuberance was evident.

In those first years, I had high hopes that we would blend our hearts together with a love for the wilderness, take joy in God's glory in creation, and bond even in their teenage years. But my zeal to cover the miles and conquer the next mountain overwhelmed the common sense to do it at their pace.

My oldest son's backpack was too heavy for another full day on the trail, so we wisely opted to pull up a little short. Backing off Dad's third-day goal gave both of us a little pleasure as we walked in the crisp mountain air and took in a beautiful day. If only I had wised up and enjoyed every day the same way.

Before we took our exit, we crossed paths with an insurance agent from Atlanta. He was rattled. On Yellow Mountain the day before, after being in the backwoods for five days, he had come face-to-face with a black bear. Most backpackers carry a whistle with them, at least in their gear. Proper protocol is to keep one around your neck or in ready access on your backpack in case you meet large game wildlife like a black bear.

Our friend had been well prepared. He had his whistle right where it should have been, but his shoulder straps on his backpack had it in a bind. He fumbled on the outside and panicked on the inside as the bear came down the mountain right at him, apparently unaware that he was there.

Eventually it did turn away, but not before it had frayed the man's nerves and melted him down. He was still shaking when we met him. He was more than ready to get back to town. The wilderness had that effect on many who took a trek into the backcountry. One bad experience can knock the wind right out of a man.

My only black bear encounter came the following year, and it was in every way a contrast to our friend's experience. I was crunching leaves at a good clip under blue skies with yellow foliage flying everywhere, all the while thinking: Wow. How could it be any better than this?

Then it happened. Just as Appalachian Trail hikers in the north look out for moose, those in the south are aware of the possibility of black bear. My eye spotted what I will call a yearling. The little fellow was no more than a year old. He may have weighed a hundred pounds (which is not much for a bear). The coal black fur combined with the golden yellow leaves on the tree he was in and the blue skies above were dazzling.

When he heard me coming, the little bear skidded forty feet down the majestic hardwood with a black trunk. He hit the forest floor with a thud about twenty-five feet down below the ridgeline. That little fellow ran downhill for all he was worth until he was out of sight. With the crunching of those leaves under my feet, he must have thought an army was coming his way.

The Boots Tell the Story

In the fall of the second year, I invited a friend to take a short trek. His experience was limited, but his heart was in it. He had purchased new boots and assured me that they were broken in. You can predict the result. We did all of twenty-one miles that weekend.

The one night we stayed on the trail, we pitched a two-man tent. We talked until the stars came out and the sounds of the night echoed in our ears. It was tranquil. In the quiet of the night air, we were solving all the world's troubles there in the heart of the wilderness. That is, until the screech owls cut loose.

He said, "What's that?" If you know how those little predators sound, you can imagine how nerve-racking it was when he was not use to hearing a forest critter cry out like a screaming child or a wailing woman. For such little creatures of the night, they could sure make a man tremble.

About midnight a harmony of snores replaced the screech owls' disharmony. We made it through the night, but my partner's feet could not make it another day. I was forced to pull up short of another elusive goal.

We came into Rainbow Campground near Franklin, North Carolina, and the lady proprietor looked down at our boots and just shook her head. One pair was gray, new, and a bit scuffed up, while the other was brown, very old, and threadbare on top. Hikers learn quickly never to take a new pair of boots on a strenuous trek like the Appalachian Trail without first breaking them in for at least a few days to form them to the feet. Mine were broken in, but to the extreme—they were also broken down and worn out.

That was no way to hike 2,176 miles to Maine. It was slow and expensive accessing the trail for such a few miles of progress. At such a pace, it would take me forty years to get to Mount Katahdin, the end of the long trail.

Shake, Rattle, and Roll

The trail provided the kind of life experiences that could make anyone shake and rattle. The important thing was finding a way to roll on so I could add miles and climb mountains on this ambitious trek across fourteen states. Many begin, but only the determined finish.

When I added up the miles at the end of that second year, it came to only 104 miles with just 2,072 to go. Something had to change, but it would take two more years before I could add the big miles.

The trail had a way of shaking you down to giving up or getting grit. And you can't get grit by reading and dreaming over a Backpacker magazine. The goal and resolve were just as real as ever, but the cost to get there was becoming increasingly clear with every passing year.

This crazy adventure meant vacation time away from the family and taking dollars from the family's limited budget. Then there was the cost to the body. Though racking up the miles made for great fitness, it also left a few injuries for the wear. Yet none of these factors could silence the call of the wilderness and the challenge of climbing another mountain.

The dreams I had in my teen years had been immersed in the hard realities of mountain travel in my thirties. There were some treasures to remember from those first one hundred miles, but after three trips the progress felt like inches. It was by inches on a map.

The biggest adjustment was missing my boys and time with them in the wilderness. It was going to be a long and tedious trial to Maine. Only those who really want it ever make it. If I had been a more patient father, we may have gone all the way. In those tender years, they could not hear what I heard crying in the mountain wind. In fact, very few did.

Raining Glory

Driving the curves of the Tennessee mountains,
golden leaves, reds and oranges, blur the skies.
They fall across the highway, mixed with rain.
Mountain rivers run strong as I drive along.

The temperature drops to icy cold at the trailhead.
The climb up is literally breath taking.
Autumn's glory is still evident even in the rain.
Then after an hour or so, the blue skies roll in.

The forest is swept with rippled color.
Across the ridges of the rugged Appalachians
the drama of God's paintbrush unfolds.
Quietly, my boots slide up and down the golden trail.

I halt on a rock outcrop to see the panorama.
My eyes run for miles down to a glassy lake,
down to dotted houses sprinkled in the deep vales.
My mind files this moment for all those tomorrows.

Cameras and videos can capture just a part of this.
It takes a hike, letting the leaves slap at your face,
catching your breath on a vista—if you want it all.
These sacred times feed the soul with God's own food.

Things You Learn Not to Do

1. Don't access the trail by United States Forest Service (USFS) roads. Stick to securing rides and shuttles from pavement.

2. Never carry cans of food in your pack. The only thing worth the weight may be a small plastic jar of peanut butter. (The further I went north, even that was not true.)

3. Do not take shelter near a road. You may get harassed and lose much-needed sleep.

4. Never hit the trail without a couple of packs of moleskin. It serves as an extra layer of skin when you have blisters. You will have blisters, unless you are a master of packing light and you have great boots.

5. Don't go very far without a good water supply. It is an obvious lesson, yet it was surprising how many got into trouble on this point.

6. When coming into town for lunch, pass on large amounts of burgers, fries and milkshakes, or you may end up eating them all over again climbing up the next mountain.

7. Do not take the hazards of rocks and roots lightly, or you will be foot sore and have blue toes.

8. One hiking stick utilized on rough terrain may throw your knees out. Use two trekking poles instead.

9. Don't take a partner who has not counted the costs of blisters, long hours of walking, a load on the back, and cold nights.

10. Never count on clear summits, daily sights of rare wildlife, no rain, all sunshine, clearly marked trails, and flat terrain.

What May Surprise You

1. The generosity of hikers, townspeople, and rangers will renew your heart for the kindness of strangers.

2. Rainy days have some of the hidden treasures of nature.

3. It feels so good to get your body in rhythm with an eighteen-mile hike.

4. There is real gratitude for trail maintenance workers, volunteers, and the Appalachian Trail Conservancy, who have given so much to the next generation of hikers.

5. A shower feels so nice after five or six days on the trail. Ahh.

6. There is absolute beauty as spring wildflowers stand out like heavenly sentinels along the trail. Then there is the stunning color range of autumn foliage.

7. Many of the delights of the trail are found in adjoining towns where people have such rich biographies.

8. There is the great joy of solitude—walking for hours and days alone in the wild.

9. It is remarkable how memorable the conversations are—though few and far between. They somehow go beyond the superficial.

10. The big surprise is how much culture, beliefs, values, and even politics are reflected on the trail. There is a strange mix of paganism and decency that ambushed me. (That is, though most hikers are kind in every way, an amazing percentage do not have a definitive faith, nor do they see the wonders of the Creator in the wilderness.)

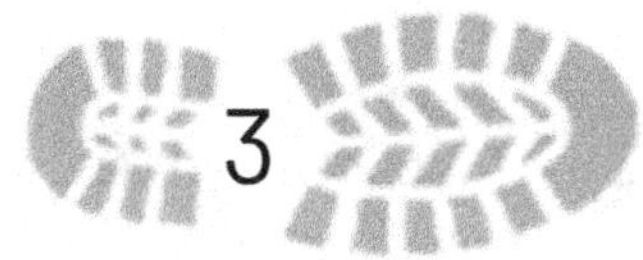

PURGING THE SOUL

I was always inviting people to the trail. The third year, a former Florida neighbor and his daughter joined my youngest son and me in November. It snowed. No, we didn't get very far, and the hikers were not the hearty kind who racked up the miles, but we had fun.

Hiking always has provided for me a purging of the soul. Even when I was a child, taking a walk in the woods, down a country road, or out across the open meadows had a way of setting the world right. When we had a young family, treks to state and national parks had the same effect on us. The snowy trek to Fontana Dam was all that and more.

In those early days of spring, we crossed paths with bear hunters and their dogs. This was often a challenge for hikers. How do you deal with hunters on the trail? I have also met grouse and turkey hunters using the Appalachian Trail. It is a little unnerving—so most hikers pull out their brightest colors during hunting season in order not to be mistaken as big game. Though I have been a hunter myself, somehow hunters and backpackers sharing the same trail did not sit well with me.

One early morning, years later in the Pennsylvania Highlands, I met a thru-hiker named, *Wild Turkey.* Right after I said goodbye to him, I met a turkey hunter. He had gnat netting over his head, camouflage fitting the woodlands, and a shotgun resting over his arm. I warned him that behind me were four other hikers and to take care. Like most hunters, he was kind and considerate. Though, there was one in North Carolina who, after I greeted him, swung his gun barrel in my direction and grunted as he turned away.

The White Wilderness

Back to the Fontana hike, the snow that November day kept pouring down in great flakes from gray skies. Those twenty-one miles to the Little Tennessee River near Fontana Dam were spectacular. We took two days to cover it. At times we were up to our knees in snowdrifts. The children, both nine-year-olds, didn't mind the hiking because they tossed snowballs and romped in the white untracked wilderness.

Even the cold didn't bother us. It was refreshing for the soul and put smiles on our faces. Unchecked laughter rang out from those white mountains. Crossing icy brooks and looking up at evergreens heavy with snow, filled us with a sense of awe and wonder. Winter had a beauty all its own

That was the last time my youngest son was on the trail; the oldest never returned either after the second year. Football became his priority, while his brother thought to average so many miles a day was unreasonable. Who could blame him? I would have to find other prospects and do a lot of solo treks before I would find a partner who loved it as much as I did. It had begun as a family project with high hopes of hiking the trail as father and sons. But that was more Dad's idea and not one the boys shared.

My wife preferred I not be out there alone because I had been an insulin-dependent diabetic since I was twenty-seven. Her concern had always been that if the blood sugar dropped due to an insulin reaction (taking too much) combined with heavy physical exertion (which also lowers the blood sugar), I would pass out with no one there to help me. That was one motivation for seeking hiking partners.

We discovered by many trials and many more errors that very few had the driving ambition to do the Appalachian Trail, especially on the 14-year plan. Most saw it as madness, an incurable disease of the mind.

There was a time when crossing a thoroughfare, while backpacking on the trail, that I met a businessman in a little convenient store near the Shenandoah National Park. I was there to replenish snacks and edibles. He looked at me and said, "I wish I was doing that." I wasn't so sure he would if he really knew the price of reaching such a demanding goal.

That third year, for the little time we spent on the trail, we saw bluebirds, a doe and fawn in the spring, a chipmunk or two, grouse, titmice, and squirrels galore. We met folks from Georgia, Illinois, Michigan, Maine, Kansas, Missouri and Alabama.

The trail was full of hikers in the spring, often in large groups, doing a few miles from gap-to-gap across the mountain passes. But the November winter trek numbered only two dads and two nine-year-olds along with the season's bear hunters with their trucks, dogs, and shotguns.

Section hiking may be hard when it comes to the logistics, but taking in the views of the trail in all kinds of weather and in different times of the year distinguishes it from the experience of thru-hikers, who make the trail their life for 5 to 6 months. For a section hiker, the adventure stays fresh, and it becomes a source of vivid memories in short spurts of time.

Once I met two brothers, Canadians, who had started at Katahdin, the northern terminus, and went southbound, hiking the northlands in the winter. They were hearty, well prepared, not in a hurry, and very reserved. For them, those days around Fontana must have been typical since they had walked in the sleet and snow for countless days.

Walking in the white wilderness with no tracks has a way of making you feel fully alive as the big flakes covered the woods and spread a white blanket over the world, hiding all the dirt and grime for a little while. Such times have a way of warming the soul of a man, even though it is very cold outside. The world for those moments was at peace. My mind could rest. Somewhere down in my heart something broke for me and a smile crossed my weatherworn face.

Two Brothers in the Wet Smokies

It was spring again. In the following year, I recruited two brothers to hike from Fontana Dam up into the Great Smoky Mountains National

Park. As usual, I was over ambitious. What I didn't count on was rain and a mountaintop thunderstorm. The brothers were physically fit for their age. They were 55 and 60 years old. One carried an old Army knapsack with an external frame for his pack. They both were experienced woodsmen.

We had a 12.4-mile climb straight up with a few switchbacks. Rain poured down the entire time. The music minister and his wife from the church where I was pastor had dropped us off at the trailhead.

The church was right in the thick of controversy. I had been there three years, forewarned that it was a "hornet's nest" and even "a graveyard for pastors." I loved a challenge. Hiking the trail was a lot easier than shepherding less-than-happy sheep. All the heartache had been building up for me, so as the rain began to come in waves of intensity, I purged my heart and mind. We pulled the ponchos on and pointed our boots uphill.

In the first few miles, the younger brother forged ahead with enthusiasm. Soon he fell back, and I took the lead. I kept glancing behind me to be sure I did not get too far ahead. We climbed all morning, walking in water running like a creek bed down the slopes we were scrambling up. The weather would break, and we would take off the dripping ponchos and fold them up or hang them on our packs to dry out, only to put them back on within five minutes when the rain would begin to pour once again.

Out peeked the sun, and then the monster clouds would cover it up and send down a deluge. After we had clocked about three or four hours, I knew it was déjà vu. Here were two brothers—much like my sons had been, at the mercy of the preacher's idea of adventure.

They had come with the high hopes of taking some great snapshots, exploring the woodlands, enjoying the views, and telling some stories. Instead, their bones were aching, their backs were cracking, and their knees were rebelling. The quiet white-bearded older brother said, "I thought this was a hike, not a death march."

We laughed and they moaned, but I got some needed release from the pressures of a troubled church. Not too many miles later, as we neared the top of the mountain range, the younger brother said, "Lord God, if you get me off this mountain, I ain't never coming back."

There was one more line forever in my memory from that soggy day. As we strained to lift our wet boots through the mud and water, the older brother sighed in exasperation, "I want my Mommy!" She had long been gone. He might have felt he was just about to meet her again.

That night we found ourselves in a tent one of the brothers had carried up the mountain. The shelter was full of wet hikers. We didn't have a lot of prime camping spots, so we camped off the converging trails under some dead trees.

Everything I had was wet and I remember borrowing orange sweatpants for the night. They were University of Tennessee Volunteer sportswear. The three of us quickly fell off into slumber land only to awake in the middle of the night by a terrific thunderstorm crashing around the dead tree limbs over our heads.

The morning came with glorious sunlight. But the men had enough of hiking in the rain forest with an overeager drill sergeant. We used a cell phone to call for a pickup in Cades Cove, a few miles down the mountain. As we descended from Russell Field, all we had hoped for in the weekend of adventure was present: wildlife was everywhere, a grand view of the valley, birds singing across the sage fields, and most of all—clear skies.

The story of that weekend was told a hundred times in church and in town circles. I have yet to live it down. While I had added a few miles to the total, I had also lost two more hiking partners forever.

If there were any chance of finding any more volunteers, I would have to go outside of the family and the county. In fact, it would be five years before I found another partner and he was from California. Like any high-adventure, it was more fun when it was shared.

It was wonderful to purge the soul and clear the mind from the power brokering taking place in the church. Even when the skies were white with snow or gray with down pouring rain, somehow the world was set right when I walked a few miles on the mountain trail marked by the white blazes. Now it was down to solo hiking from the heart of the Smokies to the miles beyond the Shenandoahs.

> *Before the mountains were brought forth, or ever thou hadst formed the earth and the world, even from everlasting to everlasting, thou are God.* (Psalm 90:2)

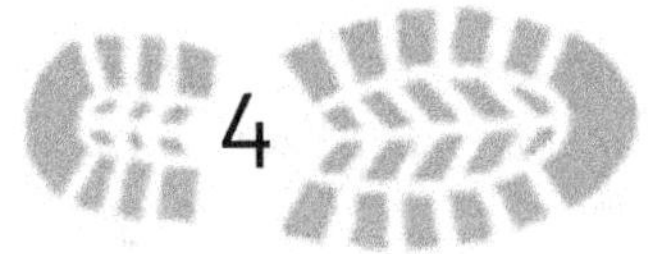

THE ULTIMATE HIKING PARTNER

It was spring in the fifth year, so I loaded up my backpack for a two-day breakaway in the Smokies. I lived close by, so instead of taking vacation time, I opted to play the weekend warrior. One month later, I added two more days for a total of 52 miles on the Appalachian Trail that spring.

Walking the Trail with Jenny

In late September I made it to Hot Springs, North Carolina, doing forty miles in three days. The last fifteen miles into the town were memorable. It was a twenty-six miles day. I saw one hunter and four hikers, and there I met Jenny.

That's what her tag said. She hailed from Erwin, Tennessee, and had a habit of accompanying hikers on the trail. Jenny was a Blue Tick hound dog trained to sniff out black bears. She had more of a nose for friendly hikers. We walked seven hours together. Jenny showed up right when I needed a little encouragement on a very challenging day.

She stayed right with me step-by-step and paw-by-paw. I fed her granola bars, and we hiked until dusk, coming down out of the mountains to a Catholic hostel. The staff there placed a call to Jenny's owner, and he came over the mountain in his muddy truck with a smile on his face. This was not the first time she had made a friend on the trail while out on a hunt.

No one else stayed in the bunkhouse that night. I managed to call my wife to tell her I hiked several hours with Jenny. Her tone changed. Then I let her in on Jenny's identity and had a good laugh.

The next morning, I had a hearty breakfast at the town café and set out for Lover's Leap Rock above the French Broad River. Before I left the hospitality of Hot Springs, I met a school boy on his way to his bus stop. He looked me up and down. "I know you're a hiker!" he said. I laughed at his boyish curiosity.

Honestly, I missed Jenny as I climbed up to Lover's Leap. She had been good company. The quiet miles went quicker with her panting there beside me, and she had no trouble keeping an even pace with me.

A month later in late October, on the fourth trip that year, I back-packed another two days and thirty-seven miles and came into Sam's Gap on US 23 along the Tennessee-North Carolina border. Hiking two days at a time was rough—by the time you get started, it is time to quit again.

The total that year with two quick trips in the spring and two short ones in the fall, over a time span of nine days, was 129 miles. All of it was solo hiking, except for those fifteen miles with Jenny.

Finally, I begin to see a little progress. As I added up the miles, I also added happy adventures that gave me much for reflection as well as inspiration. It cost a little to hike the backbone of the eastern seaboard the way I did it, but the payback was worth it all.

Sometimes after dusk with the headlamp shining in the dark shelter, I would take a pen and write a few lines while the day's experiences were fresh or jot down a thought and come back at a later time to complete it.

Becoming One Across the Miles

Walking with the wind and sun
over a harvest of acorns and chestnuts,
feeling both sweat and raindrops fall,
I am walking in the cloudland with you.

While humidity soaks me up and down,
humility works in my heart and mind.
The hours mount up and the miles add up
while you work your lofty ways in me.

Many dreams are broken in the crucible,
and hopes are reduced to but a few.
I listen in the heart of the wilderness.
Aspirations, a cut above, begin to form.

Mountains speak with the cry of the hawk
and the spirited huff of the whitetail buck.
You speak peace to me and plow deep
on the inside as you work to make us one.

Whispers from the Creator

Much of the experiences and the life lessons I took home from the Appalachian Trail were spiritual ones. Most of the people I met in town and on the trail did not put a lot of stock in the spiritual dimensions of life. For me it wasn't Zen Buddhism, New Age philosophy, or a mix-match of my own religion. It was historic Christian faith based on a literal view of the Bible, even to the point of believing in creationism.

Believing that God created the world in six days was contrary to all the natural exhibits along the way and much of the science a reader would find in the trail guides. Although I didn't have a human companion or man's best friend on many of the long stretches, I did have the very real presence of God.

Climbing mountains had multiple applications to real life. True success in life requires tenacity, traveling lightly, checking your attitude, making the best of personal encounters with people, and stretching the body and mind for the benefit of the soul. Without the challenge of reaching life's mountain peaks (worthy and sometimes painful goals), it is easy to sacrifice the soul for the pleasures of the body and overload the mind with news, information, and entertainment.

In that sixth year, I started out with 313 miles behind me with only 1,863 to go. It had taken twenty-eight days to cover those miles with an estimated 122 more days to go before I could stand on Mount Katahdin in Maine's northern woodland.

That year I backpacked from Sam's Gap to Dickey Gap in a twelve day stretch over 189 miles just after the end of winter. It gave me a real taste of trail life going through towns like Erwin, Tennessee, and Damascus, Virginia, and seeing places like Mount Rogers and the Grayson Highlands.

On the first day back out, I warmed up with an eight-mile climb to Bald Mountain. On top of the mountain there were beautiful views across the south, houses on the east, and a bald and grassy knoll to the north.

When I came to Bald Mountain Shelter that afternoon, I met *Chickadee* and *Honey Dew*, a couple from Michigan. They took one look at me and could tell I was fresh out on the trail. My beard was trim, my clothes were clean, and I looked eager.

It was a great start for time alone to clear my head as I walked the high places, though it was a bit chilly for hiking shorts. Altogether I had encountered eight hikers that day, grouse, the ever-playful chipmunks, and some juncos. I spent the evening hours swapping stories with other hikers. That was an adventure in itself.

That night the Michigan couple and I heard wild dogs howling all around us. We decided to move up to the top bunk of the shelter. Wild dogs were never a problem on the trail, but at night time the imagination can travel to foolish places.

As I became more of a seasoned trekker, I learned to shut out the sounds of the wilderness at night and go off into the neverland of sweet sleep. That night I rested lightly for ten hours, rose at 7 A.M. and was on the trail by 7:30 A.M.

Ervin, Tennessee

The next day I trekked eighteen miles into Erwin. I came into the Nolichucky Gorge Campground mid-afternoon. I stayed that night in a little hostel by myself. It was nice to get a shower, call my wife and daughter, and splurge on a diet Coke. It was there that I met Robert *"Junker"* Freeman, a 1996 thru-hiker. He was serving as a shuttle service for three retired teachers on their hike north. Junker would prove to be an incredible help to me in covering the craggy Pennsylvania miles in the years to come.

The campground featured a great outfitter's store. It was an idyllic setting tucked away in the mountains. The hostel was perched on the hillside with the Nolichucky River 725 yards away and the trail a hundred yards away.

That night I hit the mummy bag around 11 P.M.—late for a backpacker's shut eye. I had spent some needed time preparing messages for an upcoming Brazilian mission trip and outlining sermons for my sheep back home.

Long-distance hikers debate: Which is the "real world?" Is it doing life back home, earning a living, driving your truck, and going to the office? Or is the real world taking time in the wilderness, where your thoughts are free, your body rises to each day's challenges, and you have real conversations without living by the clock?

In the real world—off the trail, I was a pastor, so my work was to prepare people for the time when they would stand before God, as well as train them in the Christian lifestyle. On the trail, you can measure progress by how many mountains you climb and how far you travel. But in the world of ministry you cannot always see the results of your work.

My work in those years was in a small town in the Cumberland Mountains and things were slow. I was restless most of the time. Hiking the trail released some of that pent-up energy. On the trail, I sought to share my faith in a low-key, respectful manner. I found the majority of those I spoke with to be cold spiritually.

The highlights were always the people I met both on the trail and in town, but the person I spent the most time with and learned the most from was God himself. His presence and power were undeniable as I walked the Appalachian Trail. He was the ultimate hiking partner: He could stay up with me and not fall behind. He offered constant encouragement. He never complained, and He helped me when I really needed it most.

When I came in to Cherry Gap Shelter the next night, I left the quiet reflection of the white-blaze trail for a shelter full of people from everywhere. The sun had been a scorcher all day with rabid gnats on the attack. There had been some tough climbs over those fifteen miles of mountain terrain. The trail climbed out of the Nolichucky Gorge, and in the last couple of miles, topped Unaka Mountain at an elevation of 5,180 feet. I did see a bluebird and woodpecker as the sweat poured and the gnats swarmed.

Inside the shelter I met *Alaska* from Anchorage, *Cane Break* from Atlanta, *Woodpecker* from Israel, *Icehouse* from Pennsylvania, *Amazon* from Vermont, *KC* from North Carolina, *Slipper* from Colorado, and *Daybreak* from Houston.

Overmountain Shelter

The fourth day of this trip was pristine. The skies were blue and the air was full of juncos and bluebirds while the forest floor served as a playground for those fun-loving chipmunks. After twenty miles I walked up to the Overmountain Shelter, which was like a postcard of a red barn sitting above majestic valleys. It was my favorite shelter among the hundred or so that I saw on the Appalachian Trail.

It was a moment of euphoria to come to the end of the trail that day. I came around a curve on a slope to a clear spring, fed by a pipe about fifty yards from the converted barn that served as the shelter. It overlooked a big valley of rolling hills.

I promptly dropped my pack by the spring, took off my boots, and washed my feet. It was sheer relief to put on my sandals. I refilled my water bottles and just enjoyed the moments in that serene setting.

The red barn was full of hikers. It could house forty to fifty easily. There was *Pilgrim* from Virginia, *Gray Lox* from Israel, and *Dr. Rag* and his wife, *Rosy* from Nashville. Others were named *Meribear, Paranoid, Gingersnap,* and *Papa Dog.*

The day had been short on water and long on climbs. I had planned to stop at Stan Murray Shelter, but the water supply in the shelter was the pits. The Overmountain Shelter was absolutely spectacular with an unbeatable water source.

Most of the hikers went up in the loft while I opted for the front deck with a view of the vales below. Pilgrim and I talked for a while. Gray Lox liked my dinner attire and asked for a snapshot. As I recall, it was hiking shorts with long johns underneath.

It was the perfect setting to take up the pen and write a few lines:

Spring Beauties

Up the mountain footpath, winded from the climb,
I find a blanket of white snowy flowers.
These spring beauties rise from the forest ground
even before the buds have broken out on the trees.
Like dew drops of glory they promise spring
to the mountain tops, after winter's cold death.
There are millions, like waves on a foamy sea,
like the snow of winter and clouds across the high skies.
They cover the pinnacles, crowning the mountain bald
where the timberline stops, just above in grassy fields.
These beauties fill the air with promises and praise
and peace in the heights where heaven kisses the earth.

Foot Sore and Fancy Free

This mountain climbing business
is a dance for the mind,
but work for the rest of me.
Blisters smart while the knee barks,
yet I somehow climb until
the rhythm smooths the pain.

Overmountain Shelter

After a long day and a long trail with hours
stacked up pushing for the heights,
I come to a marker of a time in history:
The Overmountain Men crossed here
and went 170 miles in the dead of winter
to fight the British during the Revolution.
They won in their time and they win today
my heartiest respect and a noble salute.
Now I climb the same wilderness terrain
and round the hidden hollows they trod.
At my journey's end on this glory day
I find a nice spring for refreshment deep.
Then with sandals on and boots in tow
I come to a converted barn for reprieve.
There, spirited hikers tell their stories
while overlooking majestic valleys grand.

Walking on Top of the World

The Appalachian Trail leads to the top of our world,
akin to the skies, where all kinds of weather flies.

Rocks sit up there like a big circle of thrones.
The grass grows thick like velvet in royal palaces.

You walk the heavens, but the climb feels like hell.
You gain sweet satisfaction once you make it to the top.

The world seems mighty small on the downside,
and the wilderness is wonderful and vast on the topside.

Towns diminish. Nature's glories sing out uninterrupted.
Then silence covers everything except the birds' songs.

On top of the world, the planet looks right again:
big things are big and small things are indeed small.

Roan Mountain

On day five I felt more and more a part of the surroundings, and more fit all the time. That day's 22 miles was still hard, and it was a long trek crossing the Roan Mountain region of Tennessee. I saw 10 hikers, a black racer, salamanders, finches, robins, and more juncos.

When I ate Mexican rice and beef for dinner at Moreland Gap Shelter, I was safe and secure while the hail storm and thunder claps made a racket overhead. *Green Foot*, a 68 year-old man from Boston, and *Rawhide*, 18, from Norristown, Pennsylvania, were there. There was also a guitar-toting Minnesotan named, *Fen Rear*. He had just finished college and was planning on graduate school after the trail experience. A tent camper called, *Tin Man*, from Bradenton, Florida, sat nearby.

Kincora Hostel

The next day was Saturday. Food supplies were low, so it was time to restock, get a shower, do some laundry, and find a church Sunday morning. It was a short hike to Kincora, the hostel for hikers in the Hampton, Tennessee, region run by Bob and Pat Peoples. They were a very gracious couple who charged four dollars a night for accommodations: a shower, laundry, and place to cook.

I hiked 6 miles to Kincora in the morning. Bob took me to Hampton, 8 miles up the trail, and I slack-packed back that afternoon. Slack-packing meant leaving your backpack and carrying whatever water and snacks you needed for a day hike.

That night I bought groceries for the next few days on the trail and ate supper with *Rawhide* at a Greek restaurant, enjoying three pieces of pizza and a Greek salad.

Kincora was a bunkhouse with several sprawling rooms. There I saw *Pilgrim* and *Seiko* from Virginia, an Englishman, a German named Matthias, *Gray Lox*, *Lost Osprey* from Massachusetts, *Dead Man Walking* from New Jersey, and *Fen Rear*.

The next morning Bob took me back to town and I had a hearty breakfast of eggs, biscuits and gravy, and a large glass of milk at a local café. I hiked a mile and a half to Union Baptist Church, where Pastor Mickey Beal let me put my backpack in his office.

After a spirited church service, I was invited to have lunch with a gracious elderly couple. We went back to the same café I had eaten breakfast at that morning. My ribs were full when we pushed away from that table of fine country cooking.

The afternoon was beautiful with views overlooking Watauga Lake and dam. I thought of the people back home in the church and my family. That year I began a tradition of soliciting prayer requests from the people. They would fill out an insert in the church bulletin with the Appalachian Trail logo on it and an explanation of what I would be doing.

My wife filled out one: "Pastor, I am married to a 'preacher' myself. It's a tough job. Please pray for my family. I have three children. Thanks."

My daughter sent a note too:

> *Dad, I love you. We'll miss you a lot. Good*
> *luck. Have a fantastic trip with God. Next time*
> *I'll be there if I train with you, hopefully. I*
> *love you, Dad. I won't worry because God is*
> *always there. Dad, He's there to protect you.*
> *Guess who?*

She was nine years old that year. We talked about her hiking with me sometime. I always told her she would have to train before she could go. She had the grit and determination.

The average pace for many thru-hikers would be a 100-mile week. It would take about 21 weeks or five months to finish the entire stretch. I had just put in one week and was immersed in trail life. It only made me hungry for more.

Walking with the "Ultimate Hiking Partner" had its benefits. There was no falling short of mile markers or quitting. Things seemed to work smoother and there was a lot of intrigue to every day. Best of all, I could be prayed up and out. That is, I took time to talk things out with God. It really helped.

Such long stretches on the trail set the world right side up and cleaned out all the junk on the inside that accumulated from living by the clock and from the complications in a world where there were more people than mountains and trees. In such times you could let all that was wrong on the inside ebb away and replace it with what was good, and pure, and right.

The mountains shall bring forth peace to the people, and the little hills, by righteousness. (Psalm 72:3)

LONG DAY OUT OF DAMASCUS

On the eighth day that spring I was closing in on Damascus, the biggest trail town in the South. It was a wet Monday, fortunately just a drizzle and not a downpour. I came into Double Springs Shelter at 2 P.M. for a breather, to check the map, dry off a bit, and then press on to Abingdon Gap Shelter for the night.

The shelter had its array of characters including, *Walrus*, a New Mexican Navajo, *Sparky, Red Hair Tekia, Toe Jam* (she broke her foot in five places on Albert Mountain in NC), a Virginia couple, *Honolulu*, Andy (a section-hiker from North Carolina), and *Tin Man*. The night was chilly, so I didn't read or update my journal.

The following day I had a nice coast into Damascus, meeting a host of hikers. I came in right behind Honolulu. He had told me the night before that he took time off from teaching to walk the trail because his family had just been rocked by fatal illness. His Dad had just died of a stroke at age fifty-seven and his Mom had terminal cancer. He was originally from Ohio.

We came to the hostel called "The Place," sponsored by the Methodist Church in town. It could house forty plus hikers. Inside, I met *Sunny P* from Ohio, who walked twenty-six miles in her sandals the day before, two Canadian ladies, *Deadman Walking*, *Matthias* (an Englishman), *Arizona*, *Lost Osprey*, *Tin Man*, *Alaska* and *Eagle*, also from Alaska.

I took a bunk in one of the rooms by the window right under Honolulu. It was time to do a load of laundry and get supplies at Cowboy's Store. The owner gave me a friendly invitation the next morning for a Mount Rogers blueberry pancake breakfast. For the evening meal, I went for a salad.

It was good to be in Damascus, feel the buzz around the house, and hear a few stories. Somehow, I felt a little cabin fever right away, after being in the backcountry the week before. For me, when it came to town life or the wilderness, the wilderness always won.

As the sun began to move toward the west, I placed a few phone calls to home in Tennessee and to my folks in Arkansas. I also took a trip to the outfitter's store to check maps of the trail where I would be traveling the next few days.

Back at the hostel, hikers were milling about everywhere. I introduced myself to *Rufus* from California, *His Heaviness* from Columbia, South Carolina, *Goldilocks* from New Hampshire, and *Falcon* from Ohio.

When I got up the next morning, I shaved my "Peter" beard. Every spring around Resurrection Sunday our church hosted a community Passion Play in which I always played the role of Peter. *Tin Man* said I sure looked different afterward.

I was at Cowboy's Store by 6:30 A.M. and placed an order for blueberry pancakes (carbs to go). I shared the meal with *High Country* from Wyoming, who recounted experiences along the Appalachian Trail and the difficulty of being separated from his wife while he hiked.

It was a long twenty-eight miles day up and farther up. Rains drenched the mountains the entire time. I stopped at Lost Mountain Shelter at 1:30 P.M. for a needed break. It was way too early to quit, and I heard that a group of partiers was due in there that night, so I pressed on.

At one point during the late afternoon, I had one of those moments of despair. Crossing a road, with snow and rain falling freely, I contemplated hitching back into town to dry out. Then, just up the hill from the road crossing, I spied another hiker reading a map. We both sported ponchos to keep the damp out of our bones.

A Divine Encounter with Patch

We exchanged introductions. His name was *Patch* from St. Louis. He was going up the mountain to meet with friends who were waiting for him at the Thomas Knob Shelter. We had seven miles to go.

Patch was in his late thirties. He had been married twice and was alone again. As we walked up the mountain one of the most unusual and amazing conversations spilled out. It was one of those times Christians call "God moments."

When he found out I was a pastor, he asked some tough questions, and we began to compare our worldviews. It was April 28th. I know, because that afternoon changed *Patch's* life and it confirmed the big reason I was out there.

Patch was hungry for answers to life's puzzles. It was his thirty-seventh birthday. When Christians seek to relate their faith, many think it is like speaking another language. But, on that snowy and damp late afternoon, there was a soul ready to hear how Jesus could meet life's deepest needs and answer the big questions.

A year-and-a-half later, *Patch* e-mailed me. He reminded me that I had shared the three big questions of life: Who's your master? What's your mission? Who's your mate? He said he went over our conversation in his head as he hiked toward Katahdin.

Along the way, four others shared basically the same message with him. After completing the trail, he moved to Hawaii, where he linked up with a pastor who allowed him to live at the church as long as he went to Bible study every morning.

He said he was curious enough to "do some research and see if there was anything to all of this friendship with Jesus talk." Within a month he had "accepted Jesus as his Savior."

He went on to say, "My life is complete, as my relationship with Jesus grows stronger every day. Jesus is my Master. Reconciling people to God is my purpose."

It had all happened on a day when I was about to call it quits and go into town for the night. I had been cold and wet and a bit lonely, and then a divine appointment came. That conversation let me know I was where

I needed to be.

We came into Thomas Knob Shelter that night, as the daylight was growing dim. It was 7:30 P.M. Many of *Patch's* friends were waiting for him in the lower level of the shelter with a bottle of wine to celebrate his birthday. Among them were *Night Crawler*, *Yogi* and *Citrus*.

The bottom of the shelter was full and bulging, but there was a loft. Before I climbed the ladder, he asked me for a business card, and we parted with a firm handshake. In the loft three men from Ohio were warming up around their stove. I fired up mine and cooked oriental rice. It was very cold and I was chilled from getting wet.

That conversation with *Patch* while we walked the long trail was of the highest caliber, dealing honestly with life's questions without disrespect or arrogance. For a cold day we had a warm-hearted talk of things greater than man's adventures while backpacking through snowfall and icy raindrops in the mountains of the Virginia highlands.

Something happened there that is too rare among men: we touched the soul and we touched heaven. The encounter put fire in my bones and brought a deep humility to know that God was at work in this crazy project of mine

Mississippi: **The Trail Angel**

I woke up the next morning a bit frosty and it was late. I didn't roll out until 9 A.M. I fumbled with my stove to get the oatmeal going and hit the trail at 10 A.M. After covering eight to nine miles of mud and moisture, I met a volunteer forest ranger named *Mississippi*.

He invited me to a Forest Service cabin to dry everything out. I passed. There were many more miles to cover, and I planned to find another shelter for the night. I stopped at one shelter just off the trail to get a bite of lunch and take off the poncho. Three or four other men were holed up there, escaping the freezing rain.

After covering another two-to-three miles, believe it or not, I ran into *Mississippi* again at 2 P.M. He had walked the mountain on a series of trails that brought him to another A.T. crossing, where he greeted me the second time. He reissued the invitation to the Pine Mountain Forest Service cabin.

The word on the trail was that the shelters were full and running over due to the bad weather, so I jumped at the second opportunity. There, I dried my clothes out, cleaned out the pack, took a dip shower in an adjoining greenhouse, and changed into some clean clothes. It was 28 degrees outside and 68 degrees inside.

Mississippi had gone back to the trail, some four-tenths of a mile away. The cabin was hidden in a grove of trees off a side trail. While I got settled in and dried out, he rescued another hiker. They came in about an hour or two later. Low and behold, it was *Eagle* from Alaska. What a sweet reunion.

That night we were dry and warm. We kicked back in the bunk-style cabin cozy as could be. We had salad, nine-bean soup, crackers, popcorn, caribou jerky and dried figs. What a feast!

That was the beginning of a great friendship with *Mississippi*. He would later help me access the trail, share meals, and trade stories. He had been a thru-hiker a few years before and was an avid bicyclist, riding all across the southeast.

A few times he even surprised me by visiting our church for a service where I preached. He would quietly come in, a short man with strong features. He sported a gray ponytail. I would see him toward the back of the church and he would give me a broad smile. Later on, when I saw him, I would hear, "What do you say, *Arkansas Traveler*?"

We stayed in touch over the years, and he would write a few lines or e-mail me. He always encouraged me to keep reaching farther north until the day I could top Katahdin. Those are the kind of men I found on the trail. Hikers call them "trail angels"—ever willing to lend a hand, give a ride, or share a meal.

Eagle and Mississippi stand in front of the Pine Mountain Forest Service cabin on a cold day in Virginia.

Heart Talk with *Eagle*

The following day was my last one on the trail for the year. I had arranged for a couple to pick me up at Dickey Gap in Troutdale, Virginia. *Eagle* and I struck out the next morning at seven, leaving the comfort of the cabin for the trail.

We hiked twelve miles in the brisk mountain air. *Eagle* had sent all his cold weather gear back home, and then winter had returned with an icy bite. He wasn't prepared, so I left my bright orange deer hunter's toboggan with him. He actually sent it back once he finished the trail.

We had a warm-hearted conversation. He was a loner and was a little weary of the partiers on the trail. Oftentimes, he would avoid the shelters and tent sites and go off by himself at night to get a little peace and quiet. Somehow, we had made a connection.

Originally from Jacksonville, Florida, he had become a river guide in a land of contrasts with his own. He said he loved Alaska. He sure looked like the frontiersman. He topped out around six-foot-two with a full beard and nothing on his top notch. He was lean and trim and a real independent spirit, yet very likeable.

I was ready to get back to the family and the comforts of home, but I would miss the diverse experiences and the people I had met out there in the backcountry of the Appalachians. I would miss their stories and kindness and simplicity.

It never ceased to amaze me that when the will to go on was stretched thin and the extenuating factors of weather and trail conditions were ramped up, that was when the most unusual human and divine encounters happened. Any external hardship quickly faded in the joy of what went on in those brief kinships. More connections were made in such times than could transpire in weeks and even months of experiences in the comfort of town life.

Yet, my heart ached because of those I had met, very few had any connection with God. Foul language was common, paganism ruled in the majority of hearts, and if there was any religion, it was a mix-match of self-prescribed and evolving disbeliefs.

It was quite refreshing to meet those who opened up with searching questions and sought real answers by enjoying deeper conversations and making the link between creation and God's personal care for all of us.

When I finished those twelve days, I was thankful for the grace to cover 189 miles. It was the first time I could even come close to knowing how it felt to be a thru-hiker. Yet, I had the comfort of getting off the trail and returning another season.

Thru-hikers stay out there for four-to-six months of grueling challenges both physically and mentally. At times, they would tell me it seemed like it would never end. At other times, they dreaded the thought of going back to the "real world."

For the section-hiker like myself, by the time you got in rhythm and you could do twenty-two miles a day, it was time to get off the trail again. There was a high degree of motivation required. Yet it was in the toughest of times that the best things could happen.

Here are a few lines I penned in the dusk of the day after a long stretch on the trail. These were sacred times where God walked the mountains with me. It was more than on overactive imagination. God's timing is always impeccable. He knew full well who was out there and who would be crossing the trail.

If You Could See the Places I've Seen

Many sights fill our eyes, but few can move our hearts.
In the wilderness, lakes shimmer beneath mountainsides.
Timber is studded with buds, and the dogwood blooms.
It makes my heart sing to walk through the woodland.
My eyes swim in the reverence and rapture of it all.

Hearty Hampton Hospitality

Travel to a small Tennessee town and check out
true southern hospitality for the stranger.
You'll discover a more-than-great bunch of people
along with a host of surprises and kindnesses.

Hiking to a church for Sunday morning service,
I am met with a more-than-gracious reception.
Two offers for dinner come soon thereafter,
as if the people were fighting for the honor.

Dinner gives this backpacker a "full load" up front
coupled with a full load of supplies on my back.
I ascended the next mountain with a dancing heart
more-than-full of grace from the townsfolk below.

Watauga Colors

I climb where spring is full of life and vitality.
A lake shines like silver beneath emerald mountains.
Birds flash their color and fill the air with their songs.
The whole world seems to sing out and shout!
Nature's resurrection promise has come up on high.

Snowy Mount Rogers

Drenching rains fall and make the trail a washout.
When the rains turn to sleet, then snow, it is a relief.
The higher altitudes have a thick blanket of white.
Gloves and knit caps come out. Winds cut deep.
Freezing weather plays head games with all of us.
Winter bites. Shelters fill up. The trail is trackless.

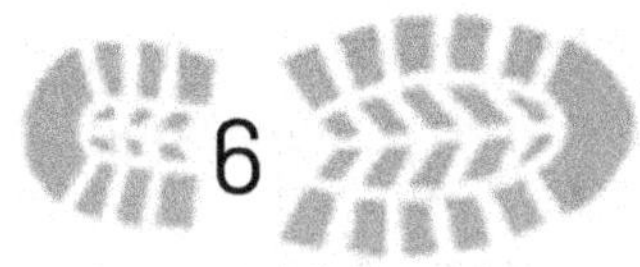

VIRGINIA TECH PIZZA

It was spring again. In the seventh year on the trail, my daughter sent me off with this note:

> *I love you and will miss you when you go*
> *on your wonderful adventure. I pray you will*
> *enjoy it and God will be with you. Love you,*
> *your daughter, Karis*

She had a habit of sending me little notes that cheered me along the way when I trekked back into the wilderness.

My wife was also a real encourager, even though the hiking adventures were costly for the family budget. She wrote this in the little Bible that I packed:

> *As you travel on this journey,*
> *Whatever be your goal,*
> *Keep your eyes upon the Savior*
> *And don't fall off a knoll.*

That spring I re-entered the Virginia highlands. Virginia has the largest section of the Appalachian Trail with 543 miles. It took me six years and eight trips to get across those gorgeous Virginia peaks. Along the way I met some memorable characters.

Here is a partial list of the hikers I encountered that spring:

Dolphin-Tennessee
Sunnybrook-Wisconsin
Super Fly-Pennsylvania
Mother Goose/Father Time- Massachusetts
Speedster-Connecticut
Grumpy-Pennsylvania
Woodchuck-New Hampshire
Chopper-Colorado
Rock Z and Zoe-Illinois
Phillip and April-Alaska
Cliff Dancer-Florida
Lady Leaper-Pennsylvania
Fenway and *Rushmore*-Georgia
Seiko-Connecticut
Red and *Rain Tree*-Tennessee
Steve and Gary-Virginia
Jess-Pennsylvania

There were a few older backpackers, but most were young and full of vinegar. It was amazing to hear why they were out there. They all had the same dream. Everyone was putting it to the test.

Hiking the Appalachian Trail was part survivor challenge, part spiritual stretching, and part craziness for the punishment hikers put themselves through on the trail. Unlike most resolutions, long distance backpacking put all of you to the test: mind, body, and soul.

Looking into the Window of the Soul

When long-distance hikers walk the trail, there are times they don't feel like making introductions. It was always a key part of the experience for me, because the people were as spectacular as the views. I liked to look into the windows of their souls and hear their stories.

I got as many names and places that I could manage without interrupting the other hiker's tranquility. Most backpackers venture into the backcountry to get a lot of thinking time. Hours of walking in the quiet woods have a way of healing the mind and putting things back in order.

Typically, I would hear an approaching hiker going southbound or find a northbound adventurer stopping for a beak. We would take about five minutes and share our stories, and I would make a mental note, so I could write it down the next time I pulled my pack off.

Most of the time trekkers were friendly and very open. People were hungry to talk about who they were and not so much about what they did. In those quick minutes of crossing the trail with another hiker, I sought to find out who they were, where they were from, and why they were out there. After all, these were the kind of people who walked where many dreamed, but few went the distance.

Six days on the trail took me as far as Pearisburg to the stopping point called Shumate Bridge, which was getting a needed repair job with heavy construction all around. Mississippi helped me with the logistics. He was working as a forest service volunteer out of Mount Rogers in southwest Virginia.

I was crossing the trail with quite a few thru-hikers. The trail was getting a lot of traffic coming out of Damascus. I added more names to my Data Book. In fact, The Appalachian Trail Data Book proved to be a great tool. It was concise and let the backpacker know where the water, campsites, shelters, roads, motels, groceries, and towns were.

It also became a record book for me. In the margins I added the names and places of origin for the hikers I met:

Manzanita-Nevada
Tex-Austin, Texas
Travis and Dustin-Iowa
Cayenne and *Hobbs*-Oregon
Buster-Connecticut
Jeff and Matt-Virginia
Forbin-New Hampshire
White Eagle-Connecticut
Packrat-Maryland
Casey-New Brunswick, Canada
Stuart and Bob-North Carolina

I also noted the wildlife I may have seen that day, the starting and stopping point, and made a notation of the number of days I had been on the trail.

In the fall I added two days and only covered twenty-seven miles. Water was scarce, and it became a factor. Water was the fuel for the backpacker. Without good water sources plans for long miles and conquering mountains literally dried up.

Beginning at the Shumate Bridge (still under construction), I climbed the hills to Rice Field Shelter which I renamed "Star Haven Shelter." It was worth the trip just to take in the sights that night. I spotted three bucks at sunset, one with a nice rack. The stars glittered and danced in the heavens.

I spent a peaceful night alone in the woodland. The shelter was at the edge of a field with a patch of woods behind it and a fence line.

Spider's Long Journey

The next morning, I met a few hikers of interest. There was *Candy Man* and *Little Debbie*. Then I spoke to *Spider* who was going 4,300 miles from Canada to Key West. He said he never purified his water, but just drank from the water source. He looked like he was out for a day-hike. Spider was light on his feet, carrying little more than a daypack, and moving in big strides with ease.

All up and down the trail, trekkers heard about two dangers that could send the long-distance hiker home. One was Lyme Disease and the other was Giardia. I had heard a few stories about gung-ho backpackers who were making great time on the trail, drank from a bad water source, and got a trip to the hospital for several weeks. I could admire *Spider,* but never emulate him.

When I geared down at the top of a mountain on a road crossing, I knew it was time to pull out because of the water shortage. I only had a few days to be out there, and after nineteen miles that day I started praying for a way back to town.

Jim was working on a Master's degree in chemistry at Virginia Tech. He was out for an afternoon drive on top of that mountain, traveling the dirt roads. I walked up to his car and introduced myself, and being a bit forward, asked him for a ride into town. He was glad to help out.

In fact, Jim became one of those trail angels. He took me into Blacksburg to his apartment and offered me a shower, which I gladly accepted. Then he drove me just off campus to a pizza parlor and insisted that I order. The Canadian bacon and sausage were delicious. I think I drank a pitcher of water.

The trip seemed like a bust, but the kindness of this stranger and student made it worth the four-hour drive from home. The short mileage was due to the extreme nature of the hike that fall. I had to go three extra miles off the trail just to find water sources.

No hiker ever reaches Katahdin by himself. There is a long list of credits for people who help him along the way: kind folks, who give rides, offer food, give a cut-rate for a motel and shower to foul-smelling back-packers, and friendly towns dotting the landscape along the way.

There are families who put up with the spirit of adventure and encourage their kin to do what few others are willing to do. Fortunately, I had that kind of family and support. Add that to the army of trail workers and rangers who kept the white-blazed trail clean and trimmed back.

Countless times I saw the fresh cuttings of volunteers who cleared blow-downs, when trees fell due to age or stormy conditions. Then there were the trail angels who kept strong boxes (wood or plastic boxes built to keep the critters out) full of fuel and food for thru-hikers at trail shelters.

At times water jugs were filled and deposited there too.

On one hand you had the dreamers who through pain and hardship became the doers on the famous footpath of the Appalachians. Then you had the dream-makers who facilitated, encouraged, and assisted so that it could happen for the rest of us who dared to climb.

Crash and *Burn*

It was the eighth year and I was on the long trail going through the Virginia highlands. Committing only five days and covering just sixty-four miles did not make it a big year for progress, but those few days provided some interesting stories.

I parked my van at a motel in Daleville and hiked back to it. Katherine Puckett, the daughter of shuttle driver Homer Witcher, filled in for her Dad and gave me a ride up the mountain. As we drove, the snow began to fall on that April day.

She asked, "Are you sure you want to do this?"

I told her, "I am committed. I have come this far and I can't turn back now."

When we made it to the top, a fresh blanket of snow covered the trail. I thanked her and paid her the shuttle fee. When I broke the trail, I felt somewhat like a mountain man traveling where no one had been.

The fact was no one had been on the trail that morning. My boots were the first set of tracks in that virgin snowfall. There was an excitement about hiking alone in the white wilderness, but I knew there were other hikers both ahead and behind me because it was prime hiking season.

The backpacking stove fired up that night at War Spur Shelter where I met *Crash* from Lynchburg, Virginia, and *Burn* from Nashville, Tennessee. *Moon Showers* from Kentucky was also there. *Crash* and *Burn* were thru-hikers, as was *Moon Showers*.

The first two were young ladies bumping twenty and *Moon Showers* was a young man, just a little older. *Crash* and *Burn* told me their story. They were very entertaining. They were also tenacious. As previously noted, when a male friend pulled off the trail after a few hundred miles, the girls had kept going.

They made a great pair. They were hardy. By the time I met them, they had adapted to the trials of the trail. No doubt their story can be repeated over and over. It is not the strength of muscle that gets you there, but of the will.

Many young and athletic young men failed to finish the dream of hiking the Appalachian Trail. They fell short because of boredom or loss of will—while children, the elderly, so-called handicapped like Bill Erwin (who hiked the entire trail blind), and many women prevailed because they really wanted it.

The strength of the will develops the strength of the muscle, and these girls had it. They could take on the mountains and hike eight to ten hours a day with a load of thirty-to-forty pounds on their backs, and do it again the next day. There was no doubt in my mind that they would go all the way to Maine.

Now a word about *Moon Showers*: I passed him the next day on a rugged section where backpackers were required to climb over boulders. He was having a hard time with the climbs—but he was talking himself over them. I admired his steel. He took it at his own pace and got it done.

Rich Personalities and a Wealth of Stories

When I came to Dragon's Tooth, a granite rock outcropping, a couple of days later, spring was more evident. I met *Strider* from Virginia and several section-hikers from Tennessee and Virginia. That night at Niday Shelter, I ate my dehydrated supper along with *DNA Dave* and *Teasel* from Vermont.

They had gathered plants from the forest and mixed them with pasta for a great home brew. They offered to share, but I was full. They were in their sixties and a real inspiration. *Wakes the Dead* from New York was another thru-hiker present that night beneath the ridgeline.

As the week moved along, the hikers increased along the trail. One day I met eighteen altogether. The day I passed Tinker Cliffs I saw *Running Bear* from Maine, *Cheerios* from Virginia, and *Havilah* from Colorado. She explained her name came from Genesis 2:11, a place noted for its gold. When I said, "Goodbye," I felt like I had met an "angel."

That was the fifth day and I came off the trail right by the Best Western Lodge, where my van was parked. It always felt good to come out after a refreshing time in the wild. Though it was a short trek, it was all the time I had to invest that year. Just think what I would have missed if I had not gone.

Every trip to the highlands paid for itself with rich experiences and further resolves to keep on adding up the miles. I knew sixty-four miles a year would never cut it. That would be the last year of small investments.

Yet even those short jaunts in the woods made for adventures to smile about: Meeting a Tech student on top of a mountain gravel road to laughing at the antics of *Crash* and *Burn* to the quiet spirit of *Havilah*. They all became part of the tales of the trail, and I was all the richer for looking into the windows of their souls.

Who hath measured the waters in the hollow of his hand, and meted out heaven with the span, and comprehended the dust of the earth in a measure, and weighed the mountains in scales, and the hills in a balance? (Isaiah 40:12)

MONTEBELLO BUNK AND BREAKFAST

It was my first two-week stretch on the mountain trail. Beginning on April Fool's Day, I hiked 210 miles in Virginia from Daleville to Thornton Gap near the Skyline Drive. The famous drive crosses the Appalachian Trail some forty times. I estimated before the trek that there would by ninety-one hours of hiking to reach the goal of Elkwallow Gap. In the end, I fell shy by 8.6 miles.

I made note of points of inspiration along the way in the back of my Data Book. Those little inspirations came from conversations on the trail. They came from a break in the weather when the rains held off or when the wind brought relief from the heat of the day. As every long-distance hiker knows, you look for ways to stay encouraged the same way you look for good water sources.

Kat and Sparrow and Frog the Dog

That first day, I found my inspiration for the day at dusk after a five-mile hike to the Fullhardt Knob Shelter. There I met a couple named *Kat* and *Sparrow*, a young husband and wife from Harrison, Arkansas. Close by was their dog, Frog. They were south bounders.

As we talked, we discovered that we shared a common faith. After a lively conversation, they opened their two-person sleeping bag and crawled in, and then Frog climbed in between them. It was a frosty night, and they all stayed warm.

They wrote me later in the year to say that they had reached Springer Mountain. Attached was a photo of two pairs of feet and one pair of paws standing on the bronze plaque in Georgia that marks the end of the trail for south bounders and the beginning of the trail for north bounders.

The next day I went north while my animal, bird, and amphibian friends went farther south. It was a challenging day of nineteen miles to the Cove Mountain Shelter, where I spent the night solo. During the day I had met hikers from Virginia, South Carolina, and one *Lion Heart* from Fresno, California.

There was no water at the shelter, so I had to bring in an ample supply for supper and breakfast. That is one sticking point for every backcountry adventure: be sure of the water supply and don't pass up streams too quickly before checking what is available the next few miles.

A Cold Night and Hot Hospitality

Day three was a little over sixteen miles into Thunder Hill Shelter, which was within easy walking distance of a road, not the best place to be for backpackers. We prefer to stay away from the traffic and the unpredictable nature of man, but on this night, it worked to my advantage.

It was a below-freezing night. The three other men I shared the shelter with had put up big green tarps to block the chilly wind. They hailed from New Jersey, a father and son, and the father's friend. They had just been to a West family reunion in, of all places, the town I ministered in—back in East Tennessee.

They were on the road, and their truck was less than a few hundred yards away. We got to know something about each other—and then they started cooking. That night I had steak, jalapenos, cheese, tomatoes, and chocolate.

Dawn broke with frosty and shivering temperatures. I said farewell and turned my blue face to the north. Covering a little over seventeen miles, ascending a couple of hard hills, I came off the trail early to John Hollow Shelter at 3 P.M., a bit foot-sore.

It was a quiet night all by myself. I took in a trail favorite of macaroni and cheese before climbing into the warm sleeping bag. Sleeping on the trail is considered rough for some because it requires sleeping on hard wood without the comforts of home. But one of the pleasures of the back-country was to bed down before nine and rise around six. It was great to get a good night's rest after a long day of exertion.

On day five, I met a rich diversity of personalities on the trail. Hiking seventeen miles, I encountered twenty-three Boy Scouts, and thru-hikers: *Caesar* from Miami, Florida, and *Maude* from Connecticut with their dog, going south.

Caesar was an insulin-dependent diabetic like me. They had been on the trail for nine months and were raising money for diabetes. We compared notes while they ate lunch beside the trail. They had taken several "zero days" off the trail to attend family events and see some sights before returning to the rigors of living out of their backpacks.

Ottie Cole Powell and the Slave Camps

Before I called it a day, I came upon the little grave of Ottie Cole Powell, a four-year-old schoolboy who got lost from his schoolmates. He had wandered seven miles before he fell to the earth and died. They found his body the next year up on the mountain.

All afternoon my imagination had been pondering the history of the region as I walked along the small ridges where brooks rumbled beside me in the last hours of daylight. These trails, running beside little river-banks, had been a refuge for slaves released in generations past. I could almost hear their voices and see the children playing near the rippling water while the women folk did their wash. The only place they could find peace from the disparity of the age was the wilderness where they could eke out a living.

At least in the woods and along the brooks they had equality and equity.

Thinking of the voices of the children playing along those natural waterways made my face smile though my heart was sad. If only men could wash clean from the dirt and grime of hate.

Medicaid Charlie and *Medicaid John*

When I pulled off my pack at Brown Mountain Shelter, I introduced myself to *Medicaid Charlie*, age seventy-three, and *Medicaid John*, age seventy-five. John had hiked the entire trail a few years before. He had knee replacements and perhaps a few other parts. He had become a hero in his hometown for his accomplishment.

These old timers were feisty and spirited, averaging about eight miles a day. The privy was straight up a hill behind the shelter and you should have heard John gather up his courage with his roll of toilet paper in tow. Meeting those two left no room for complaints from those like myself who still had a measure of youth.

They poked fun at each other and took on the dynamics of the trail together and somehow overcame all the obstacles. It made me realize that heroes are often the least likely candidates. They inspire because they have the grit and humor to beat the odds that defeat so many others who have their original parts and much more youth.

Charlie and John were "old" men, but they had young hearts. What was on the inside carried what was on the outside. The pleasures they found on a eight mile hike every day superseded all the pains and inconveniences. That is how they kept young while most men their age were sitting in Lazy Boy recliners.

Montebello, Virginia

Saturday morning broke with the promise of a shower somewhere in town that night. It was my practice to find a church on Sunday, so I hoped to get into Montebello by dusk. Crossing eighteen miles of beautiful mountain terrain, with a little navigation work, brought me to civilization.

I met a few day-hikers and an interesting middle-aged adventurer named *Backtracker*. He was actually hiking every section of the trail by leaving his vehicle at a road crossing, hiking the distance and returning in the same tracks back to his vehicle.

His plan was to hike the entire Appalachian Trail in that fashion, covering it both ways all the way to Maine. We hiked a couple of miles and then prayed together before parting. It put me in mind of my twelve-year-old daughter's note that I carried with me:

Dad,
Have a great thirteen days. I will be praying for you every step
of the way. I will also pray you'll be safe, but have a blast? (She
placed the question mark there.) And I know you'll meet all sorts
of people to share God with them. Sometimes I think God puts
you out there for that one purpose, to share God. Much love and
prayers, your daughter, Karis

After buying a few supplies at the store in Montebello, I inquired about a place to stay. They referred me to Dutch Haus Deselligkeit, hosted by Earl and Lois Arnold. The bed and breakfast were both reasonable and delightful in every way. What a place!

There were all kinds of books on the outdoors along with nice, comfortable furnishings throughout the house. It was there that I became acquainted with the paradiddle, a small red mountain squirrel that resembles the chipmunk without the spots. The little fellow was known to be very aggressive and fiery in demeanor.

The Arnolds filled me in on the exploits of the paradiddle. They were known for finding their way into an airtight house. When they watched them through the windows of their sitting room (which also served as a dining room for their guests), the paradiddle wanted the run of the entire back yard, scattering all the competition for the bird feeders and bread crumbs on the ground.

Years later and with a little research, there appears to be no veracity to the paradiddle stories. There is no record of such a squirrel or animal in Virginia or anywhere else (except in the first edition of this book!). I got snookered by the tales of a mythical critter. They had taken me on a long snipe hunt.

It was wonderful to get a shower—a long and hot one that steamed up the bathroom. Then add to that: clean clothes after my dirty laundry was returned to decency. Supper was superb. I shared it with a young couple: Alex, who was originally from Quebec, and Jennifer, whose home was in Texas. Both were lawyers from Washington D.C., about five hours away.

After a cozy night in a bunk bed and private room, I sat down for a feast at breakfast: a cup of tea, quiche, bowl of fruit, waffles made from sweet potatoes, and juice.

Then a prearranged meeting at the country store (where I had purchased supplies the night before) linked me up to Madeline, an older lady, who took me to Mount Paran Baptist Church for their morning worship service. The people there were very friendly with this rough backwoodsman, even though I was cleaned up a bit.

I was on the trail by 2 P.M., passing some nineteen hikers before coming into Harpers Creek Shelter after ten miles. That Sunday afternoon I journeyed for two to three miles with Jim (a PhD) and, at the time, a second-year law student. When crossing a road later on, I came upon a plastic bag marked with my name and a note:

> *So enjoyable meeting you at Mount Paran.*
> *Praying for you to have a safe and fantastic*
> *journey.*
> *Happy trails, Vern and Cheryl Simpson*

Inside the bag were a dozen nut-laden chocolate brownies. Talk about a sugar rush and calories to go. Wow! I ate what I could and left the left-over blessings wrapped and hung in the shelter that night.

Waynesboro, Virginia

In week number two the trail was becoming a little like home. I was finding my hiking rhythm and taking in the trail culture. On day eight the target was Waynesboro, a twenty-four miles jaunt. I didn't get into the motel until after dark. There was only one noteworthy thru-hiker that I crossed paths with that day. His name was *Against the Flow* from Richmond, Virginia.

Though it had been only two days since I was off the trail, it still felt good to get a shower, order pizza, salad, and drink a Mountain Dew. I called my wife and talked while I stretched out on the double bed with backpacking gear lining the walls.

On Tuesday morning I had breakfast at the inn and bought supplies at a Chevron station before hitting the trail. It was a wet day—very wet. I felt like packing it in—I couldn't see anything on those muddy mountain trails but my soggy boots, because the poncho blocked all visibility.

In sheer misery, I pulled off the poncho at one point, unbuckled the pack quickly, and unwrapped a Nutrageous candy bar while the rain poured down. My blood sugar had dropped without me realizing it. The nutty chocolate bar with a peanut butter base sent a surge back into my weak and weary body. I felt like I just stepped out of a telephone booth with a red and blue cape.

After twenty soggy miles I found the Blackrock Hut at 6:15 P.M. Somehow, I managed to get acquainted with *Flyboy*, *Wounded Knee*, and *Wildfire* in route along with another thru-hiker called *Terranaunt*.

Skyline Drive Country

On day ten, everything changed dramatically from the day before. This was Skyline Drive country, which I crossed repeatedly. Instead of rain and an endurance contest, there were natural wonders and a host of wildlife to take in under blue skies.

Three sets of hikers were on the trail, including a father and daughter from Cape Hatteras, North Carolina. Their names were *Driftwood Dog* and *Salamander*. Before I took off my boots at Hightop Hut, I also introduced myself to *Hog-on-Ice*, who was hiking south on the white-blaze trail.

The twenty-one miles that day closed out in style with a herd of deer grazing nearby, and crows calling out along with a gorgeous mountain sunset on the edge of the woodland. I was alone but quite content that night. Every soul needs such times for reflection, just to let the stillness at the end of the day seep into the cracks and crevices of the heart.

The two-week trek was winding down. It was Thursday morning and another beautiful day (just think if I had quit on that dreary Tuesday). Hiking just twelve-and-a-half miles into Bearfence Mountain Hut was a nice break. I came in early, gave my feet a needed rest, and enjoyed the rock shelter with a spring-fed water source up front.

Lunch had been a pleasure that day with mini-cracker sandwiches and GORP (an acronym for "good old raisins and peanuts," a trail mix that may also have M&M's and yogurt pieces), and a call home by cell phone. In the afternoon, a couple of military jets had cut across the skies above the wilderness tree line at Mach speeds.

Once again, I had the place to myself. Kicking off my boots for sixteen hours was pure ecstasy, in addition to getting needed rest, I took joy in watching the day fade away quietly.

The dawn came, and I packed up for a sixteen miler to Skyline Lodge, stopping for lunch at Big Meadows Wayside.

The shower, dining room supper, and little suite overlooking the Appalachian woodlands at the Lodge were great. The views were spectacular.

More than any place on earth, I love the blend of mountains and forest set against a late day horizon. There was such peace and solitude. It beat a pristine beach anytime. The smell of the forest and the sound of a chorus of crickets, joined by songbirds at the end of the day, filled my heart with wonder. What a fine way to spend the last night.

On the final day in the wilds of northern Virginia, I walked in the clouds for nine miles before I came to Thornton Gap around 12:10 P.M. There, I waited for my ride from a staff member at the church back home. It was good to be on my way back to the house after thirteen days of walking the Virginia ridgelines.

Thy righteousness is like the great mountains; thy judgments are a great deep: O Lord, thy preservest man and beast.   (Psalm 36:6)

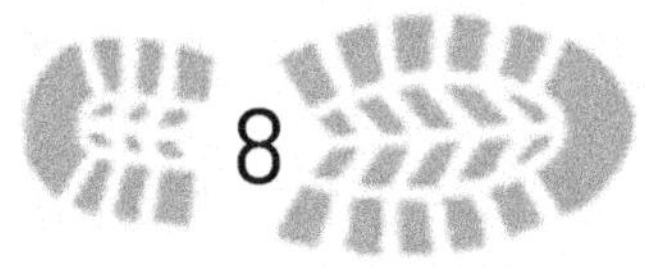

PRUNE PICKER

The forest was full of color in that ninth year on the grand American trail as I returned for the eighteenth trek, hiking north, section-by-section. This time I had the joy of having a hiking partner. No previous hiking partner had ever returned. But this one would be different.

Eric and I had gone to seminary together in Texas back in the eighties, both single and studying to be a pastor and missionary respectfully. Those were formative years, to say the least. We both married and had sons before we moved to our first ministries.

He went back home to southern California, and I moved my young family to South Florida. We stayed in touch through the years, mostly through Christmas card exchanges. After nineteen-years, we emailed each other about this crazy ambition of mine to finish the Appalachian Trail. He said he would love to go sometime, so I extended an invitation with a time and place.

He flew into East Tennessee, drove up to our little town in the mountains, and then we saw each other for the first time in almost two decades. He had changed very little, still had that wide grin and a boy's mischief. The reunion was sweet, and we quickly bonded as we had years before.

The jokes began almost immediately. He was a man fully prepared. He had trained. He had the gear. He had the want-to. While my gear was hand-me-down from my oldest son, Eric had all the most recent gizmos in the backpacking world.

The Origins of *Prune Picker's* Trail Name

Now a word about his trail name: I told him he had to have one. He thought back to our old neighborhood in Fort Worth, Texas, where we had both settled after getting married and moving off campus. There was a delightful, retired preacher who lived there.

His name was Mr. Finley. He always had a ready smile and a happy greeting as we walked to and from the seminary. Mr. Finley took care of all the neighbors by raking, sweeping, doing odd jobs, and being the neighborhood Good Samaritan for all who were in his territory of kindness.

When Mr. Finley heard that Eric hailed from California, he dubbed him *Prune Picker*. Eric laughed, and he never forgot it down through the years. So, when I asked him for his handle, he quickly retrieved Mr. Finley's affectionate nickname.

Eric came into our home and unloaded his gear. We compared packs and foodstuffs and got ready for an early morning departure the next day. All those years I had been a church planter and pastor and Eric had become a successful businessman as well as a minister.

Most pastors in rural America just get by financially, regardless of their educational level. I never felt free to work another job, so things were usually tight for us, yet God continually took care of our family. Even so, the backpacking adventures were always a sacrifice for the family.

When Eric pulled out his gear that night, he presented me with a matching set of hiking poles. I was thrilled and humbled. I had hiked with a stick in earlier years, but I found that with a single hiking stick for one side of the body, the opposite knee would be adversely affected. Thus, I abandoned it.

For a guy with just basic gear, it was a great gift to have. Almost all the long-distance hikers used trekking poles. It would be a joy to break them in together and experience the advantage of a little leverage up and down those mountains. Somehow, I felt my old friend would be able to match me step-for-step, unlike others I had invited on the big climbs.

We had four full days planned from Thornton Gap in the Shenandoahs to Harpers Ferry, West Virginia. Eric had never hiked that many miles before. He still wanted to go at my pace and do the miles we needed to do. He had no trouble keeping up.

The Uphill King

Soon we penned him with the name *Up Hill King* because of his agility on the climbs, while I was the *Downhill King*. We complemented each other in our strengths that way. Along with his gear, Eric had Gospel tracts and Scripture portions to share.

We took great joy in our fellowship and renewed friendship, as well as taking opportunity to share with those we met along the way. We faced the typical obstacles most backpackers face in crossing the wilderness, but doing it in pairs was a different experience altogether for me.

No wonder most thru-hikers find a group of four or five people that they hang with all the way up the trail. Compatibility can be a real challenge, but the right partner knows when to give you space, when to speak up, and when to readjust the itinerary. Fortunately, we shared those dynamics.

We filled out a backpacking-use permit for the Shenandoah National Park on the twenty-second of October. Our plan had been to park my van at the trailhead, the getting off spot after our four-day trek and get a ride to the starting spot at Thornton Gap.

It didn't quite work out the way we had expected. It took us a lot longer than we had estimated to get the shuttle back to the Gap. It also cost more than what we had planned.

As a result, we came to the Thornton Gap at dusk and decided it wasn't wise to make the descent to the shelter. We opted out, got a motel, had a hearty breakfast the next morning, and hitched a ride back to the trail.

That morning we pushed into the wilderness for our first seventeen miles and our first night away from the big lights. What a way to break in a hiking partner, but *Prune Picker* had the stuff. We took on Pass Mountain and the peaks of Hogback Mountain and Little Hogback.

The backpacks went off at Gravel Springs Shelter. It was a fairly nice and clean home in the wilderness near a tent camping area. That late afternoon we had a visitor. His name was Derek. He wore sackcloth and spoke in abstract religious jargon.

He was hungry so we shared some food with him. Both of us were thinking the same thing when he left. We were very uneasy. He didn't seem quite right. That night, we lay down in our sleeping bags, and at the exact same time took the tips off our hiking poles and laid them beside us.

Mice in the Shelter

That night Derek did not visit us, but the mice did. Eric was not accustomed to that. He asked me how I slept with mice everywhere. I told him they had crawled across my face before and I just rolled over and went to sleep. Most of the time I was too tired to care.

On the day before, we had met *Mini-Mosey* and a few other hikers. The second day we saw *Lady* and *Mud Lark*, crossed Highway 522 near Front Royal, Virginia, before arriving at Jim and Molly Denton Shelter. It is one of the best on the entire trail. We had it to ourselves with a shower and good water source.

It had been a nineteen-mile day. Pulling off our boots and kicking back in the nice front porch chairs the shelter provided was sheer luxury. We cooked our meals on one of our stoves and talked until the sunlight went out. The weather had been pleasant and the colors were spectacular, but that was about to change.

The third day was wet. We pulled out our rain gear. Eric had a Cabela's red rain suit. He looked like he had stepped right out of a Cabela's magazine. I had to rib him for it, though I looked like I had stepped out of a Good Will Store with my poncho and black-and-gray windbreaker.

Elvis on the Trail

We covered just ten woodland miles and came into the shelter early due to the rain. As we were unpacking our gear to let it dry out in Dick's Dome Shelter, *Elvis* walked up. There he was, just in for a few moments. The young man came from Connecticut, twenty-one years of age, the son of a Jewish mother and Roman Catholic father.

Elvis had the build of the young Elvis from Tupelo, but not the same looks. He wasn't humming or strumming, but he was unassuming like the younger Elvis was reported to be. Though he was minus the southern accent, there was nothing unfriendly or unkind about him.

He was the first hiker we had seen that day. We spoke briefly, and he decided to make a few more miles before calling it a day. Dick's Dome was perfect for two or three backpackers, but not any more. It was a gray shingled, dome-shaped structure set on concrete blocks.

The fourth day turned out to be the hardest. I underestimated the mileage, and we had to hike five more miles than we had planned. Eric was patient about the mix-up. He couldn't believe I was so cheery, singing and humming along the way. But I would come to a breaking point during that day's nineteen miler.

Bears Den Rock Hostel

We met many more hikers: *Time Bandit* and *Lost Cause* were among them. It grew dark, and we had to pull out our headlamps during the last few miles. We kept looking for signs to point us to Bears Den Rocks, a hostel in the area. We feared we might have gone past it in the dark.

As it got darker and the rain began to fall again, we stumbled to find our way on the trail, searching for the white blazes on the trees ahead. At one point, I was almost certain we spotted a bobcat ahead of us, peeling off to the left into the bush. I began to worry out loud and a little panic crept into my voice. I was feeling responsible for the miscalculated miles and meandering in the pitch dark.

On that day I was closing in on 980 miles on the trail. As with anything else, experience makes a backpacker resilient. Even so, there were breaking points—like a day of drenching rain or the uncertainty of whether or not you missed a directional sign. When you come down to the final mile of a long day (even with good company), and darkness has set in around the mountainside, you know you're close, and you just don't want to miss it by a few feet because you're stumbling in the night.

Eric was reassuring, and we gathered up our courage to see it through to the elusive hostel. Just about the time we thought we had missed the sign we came upon the marker we had been pushing for that black and wet night.

It was a real relief and we both smiled and punched each other. We walked the few yards to the stone edifice found near the town of Bluemont, Virginia. We were soaked and beat, and ready for a shower and meal.

That night was surreal. At one moment we were near despair, the next moment we were in a warm and dry place with other hikers, and hearing the songs of a church youth group upstairs. The bunkroom was just about full downstairs, but they did have a couple of spaces for the two of us.

After a shower and putting in a load of laundry, we went upstairs to share the hospitality of the youth group, complete with a large salad and pizza. We topped it off with a big, scrumptious cookie. Wow! It all tasted so good.

Eric and I joined in to sing the praise songs which we knew by heart. All we could do was smile at the turn of events. We spoke with one of the resident assistants, and she set us up for a ride to our vehicle the next morning.

We ended up falling short of Harpers Ferry, West Virginia, by nineteen miles. Altogether, we climbed and descended sixty-two miles. The directional signposts in front of Bears Den read 1,164.7 miles to Mount Katahdin and 938.7 miles back to Springer Mountain.

It was a long journey north, but we were getting there. Thanks to a great hiking partner, the years ahead would not be so grueling. I could share the incredible experiences with someone who understood the dynamic of the trail, even though he looked like he walked out of a Cabela's catalog!

As we drove back to East Tennessee from the northern reaches of Virginia, our trekking poles were a little less shiny and a little bent from the wear, but it was all good. We laughed at all the memories we had packed into five short days and set tentative plans for autumn of the next year.

Prune Picker matched me mile-for-mile. He kept an amazing attitude and provided tremendous encouragement.

ZEN MONKEY

Spring came and the call of the wild began to cry out in my spirit again. I worked out, doing two-to-four mile runs to get my heart and legs ready for a return to the mountain climbs. This time would not only be in the Virginia highlands, but along the ridgelines of West Virginia, Maryland, and rocky Pennsylvania.

Hiking alone, I added 162 miles to my total in ten days and left the southern Appalachians behind for Yankee country. It was a trip to remember. Once again, the intriguing part of the journey was the people I met while crossing three state lines.

The defining moment was one long night in Pine Knob Shelter. Yet, the positive experiences far surpassed the few negative ones. This stretch would bring me to the halfway point after ten years of section hiking for some eighty days along the Appalachian Trail.

Back at the Bears Den Hostel in northern Virginia, I left my little gray Dodge Neon in the parking lot for Robert *Junker* Freeman to drive to his home in Fayetteville, Pennsylvania, where I would pick it up. That night I bunked at the Bears Den with Sam, Dave, Stacy, *Hippie Long Stockings*, and *Southern Harp*. Lights went out about 10:25 P.M.

When the sun rose, I cooked breakfast in the kitchen at the hostel. My prayer for the next week-and-a-half was to have fellowship with the Father in the wilderness. This was an alteration to the Appalachian Trail Conservancy slogan: "The Appalachian Trail: A footpath for those who seek fellowship with the wilderness."

The first day back I hiked just eleven miles, starting out with an easy pace and breaking my body in slowly. My boots were unlaced by 2:30 P.M. at David Lesser Memorial Shelter. There I met a host of hikers. One would become a good companion in the days ahead.

On the trail that day, I stopped a few moments at the Blackburn Trail Center (a nice place to eat and sleep for a price), and spoke to Sara and Kie, the wife and daughter of the caretaker. I came upon *Lost Cause* from Vermont, a thin young man I had seen six months before on the trail, and I also met Jim from Virginia.

In the shelter I was introduced to *Papa Bear*, a sixty-nine year old from North Carolina, *Kilt Walker* from Virginia Beach (who actually wore a kilt on the trail and fought diabetes as I did), Paul from Arlington, Virginia, and his dog, Griffith, and *Zen Monkey* from Seattle.

There was also an unnamed and unprepared young man in his twenties. All of us were concerned for him. He had very little gear, no sleeping bag, little food, and no winter clothing. A rat-chewed sleeping bag had been left in the shelter, so he took it.

We shared food with him. He was not very coherent and could not tell us where he was going. He left sometime before dawn to wander the ridgelines. There were people like that out there, who were literally lost souls without direction and no idea of their need for common sense or a game plan for wilderness travel.

That first night on the trail, I got acquainted with *Zen Monkey*, an emergency room physician from Washington State. His wife was also a physician. He was into Zen Buddhism. I shared my faith with him, and we compared notes of trail life. We talked the afternoon away.

Four of us shared a dessert that night. Ah, life on the trail where total strangers become fast friends. The following day would bring me to Harpers Ferry and the headquarters of the Appalachian Trail Conservancy (ATC) where West Virginia meets Maryland.

Harpers Ferry, West Virginia

The next day, I descended into town and took the .02 mile side trail to the ATC Center, where I signeda register, was assigned a number, and had my picture taken for the 2003 album of hikers. The ranger who assisted me said I was the twenty-sixth section-hiker that year.

It was a pleasant day after a very cold night. While I was in town, I purchased a fleece liner for my sleeping bag at an outfitter's store. Going light was a priority, but staying warm and getting a good night's sleep was a higher priority.

Strolling up and down the narrow streets of Harpers Ferry, I stopped to get a hamburger and fruit drink at a cafe on my way out of town. I joined other tourists at a museum on the history of the region, where John Brown and then United States Army officer Robert E. Lee made their marks in American folklore.

There was a flat stretch along the Potomac River before I started climbing again. I was in Ed Garvey Shelter by 3:30 P.M. after sixteen miles. I saw ten hikers that day. That night the men in the shelter were from Maryland and New Jersey.

I climbed to the loft and prepared for a cold night. It was sweet and sour noodles for supper. Clad in my sandals and wool socks, I walked .04 mile downhill for water and then right back up again. I got settled in and watched a twelve-year-old youth play with the fire as his Dad cleaned up the cooking pans. Other men gulped down noodle soup and crackers, following it up with coffee. Another hiker munched on peanuts and stretched his weary limbs.

Party Dogs

Up early, I covered seventeen miles to Pine Knob Shelter. On the trail that day, I saw a lady hiker, *True North* from Oregon, along with Ken, Diane, and their dog taking on a section-hike.

I crossed I-70 right before the trail passed by the shelter. That should have been a warning sign for me. Most backpackers do not like being near a road, especially on a Friday night. It usually means only one thing:

trouble. At the shelter I squeezed in between *Screwy Squirrel* from Ohio and six other men from New Jersey. *Crazy Horse* from Las Vegas was tent camping nearby.

The small army of men from New Jersey were not hikers at all. They had invaded the shelter with a cooler of food and booze. Unfortunately, they were not only generous with their meat and cheeses, but also with their variety of toxins (not tonics).

It had been a short day, finishing the day's hike by 2:30 P.M. It was a little on the wet side. When I walked up to the simple shelter, a couple of teenage boys were tossing a football while the men laid out foodstuffs on a picnic table.

As the sun set, the men followed up a hearty meal, that was grilled on a hibachi, with strong drink. They had no shame as they indulged in front of two fifteen-year-olds. They knew I was a preacher from our conversation. They got fully loaded as night fell. We hung up our food bags and stretched out in our sleeping bags.

The dark hours began to slowly crawl by as other men came in from the tenting area. As the liquor flowed, barbs about the military were exchanged between *Screwy Squirrel*, a Vietnam veteran, and a young buck. A fight just about broke out. All the while, I was trying in vain to sleep as foul language peppered every statement. I was bunking in a saloon.

Someone in anger punched my food bag and *Screwy Squirrel* said, "Leave the preacher's food bag alone. He's all right." He was a little under the influence. Finally, after the sparks had flown, the men settled in. The old soldier climbed right on top of me and quickly apologized.

He wedged in between myself and man number eight in a six-man shelter. Somewhere around two and three in the morning I fell asleep and awoke to the pitter-patter of rain. (I had seriously considered a night hike in the rain while the drinking was going on.) Shooting out like a rocket released from the launch pad, I hit the trail early so I could distance myself from the madness of the night.

Within just a few miles, I was talking to *Alfonzo* and *Black Hawk*. It was like going from one extreme to another. These men were believers. While my heart grieved for the lost men behind me, I rejoiced to meet two brothers in the faith. We even took time beside the trail to pray.

The day before, I had talked heart-to-heart with *Crazy Horse*. He had been raised in East Tennessee where I resided. I gently challenged him in his faith. He said he liked to hike to be close to God, even though he had an affinity for cussing and gambling. That morning when I left Pine Knob, he was sawing logs in his tent at 7 A.M.

What an array of experiences. *Alfonzo, Black Hawk* and I visited for thirty minutes close to a rock outcropping, took pictures, and exchanged contact information. After I left them, I passed three groups of Boy Scouts. There were forty-one altogether, in addition to a couple of section-hikers and their dog traveling south on the trail.

When the day was done with thirteen miles completed, I unloaded my backpack at the Devil's Racecourse Shelter. It was named for a river of boulders behind the old and dilapidated log structure. You could hear the rushing water running underneath the river of boulders. A father and son, Russ and Nick, from Carlisle, Pennsylvania, were there. Zen Monkey came in right behind me. It was good to see him and catch up on the last few days. We kept building our friendship and respect for each other each time we met.

The next day was Sunday, and I would be scouting for a church just off the trail. My search was unsuccessful along three paved roads. Church services were much earlier there than down south. Altogether, I covered twenty miles that Lord's Day.

I saw Russ and Nick again at Pen Mar Park. They took a picture, which they e-mailed to me later on with a nice note. The park was on the Maryland and Pennsylvania state line. I had left Dixieland behind. There were sixteen hikers out that Sunday: a group of eight youth, four in one family, a couple of men, and thru-hikers *Soft* and *Stretch*.

Here is the photo Russ took at Pen Mar Park

Zen Monkey had written me a note and duct-taped it to a tree with a directional arrow pointing the way to a church on one state road:

"Arkansas Traveler...church one-fourth mile on road to left...*Zen Monkey."*

But, alas, I was too late for the service time.

When I unlaced my boots at one of two stopovers at Rocky Mountain Shelter, I was alone. It was a well-kept place. The water source was down a side trail right on a paved road. Though it was near civilization, the shelter was well hidden from view of the road. I spent a quiet evening there in unbeatable solitude and contentment.

Fayetteville, Pennsylvania

There was hope for a shower the next day in Fayetteville, where *Junker* lived near a state park. After a few days out in the backcountry, getting a shower was almost as sweet as a good town meal. So, the following morning I hit the trail again. Later, I linked up with *Junker*, who had been a thru-hiker himself in years past, and enjoyed a shower and breakfast in town. His hospitality could not have been better back home.

Back on the trail, I finished the day at Birch Run Shelters—there were two shelters at one spot. I met *Three-Wheel Drive, Doublewide,* and ten youth, hiking along the thirteen-mile stretch.

It was great to be alone again and get some time to pray and work through some things. Yet, I felt the ache of missing my family. I was leaning against the front of the shelter, nodding off a bit, when Joan walked up. There were definite signs of construction around the shelter sites. They were building a third shelter and she was checking on the progress the workers were making. We talked for about thirty minutes, and then she pressed on.

The water source was nearby, and I drank a lot of water. It is hard to quench your thirst after a hearty hike because the body dehydrates. I opened my Bible and read a few chapters, then prayed on that quiet evening in the middle of the wilderness. It was solace for the soul to drink it all in. The next forty-eight hours were going to be challenging, since I had to travel in excess of twenty miles each day. I enjoyed the quiet reprieve.

Tuesday dawned with promise and I set off for the first climb of the twenty-six miles that day. I passed by Pine Grove Furnace State Park, a stop famous for the half-a-gallon ice cream eating contest. It was quiet and closed when I passed by. I did meet *Lucky Dog*, Mike and *Tumbleweed*. I also had a nice chat with Chad Bupp, a fisherman there in the park. We spoke of faith and heart matters in a memorable exchange.

The Halfway Mark

There it was, just out of the park on a little uphill climb: It was the halfway mark for the Appalachian Trail. There were 1,069 miles behind me and 1,069 miles before me. It was a wet day. As I trekked past Whiskey Spring, I spied four rock climbers above me and greeted them.

The sunshine did break through. *Zen Monkey* looked like he was gone for good. He was always the entry before mine in the trail logs at the trailheads and shelters.

I reached Alex Kennedy Shelter at 4:30 P.M. For the third night in a row, I was solo. Jim and Marie came by the shelter out on a day-hike. They were a Jewish couple. Later on, when I was brushing my teeth after supper, a couple of teens, a brother and sister named Paul and Renee, came by the shelter and also spoke briefly with me.

The Kennedy Shelter was ideal with elevated bunks, plenty of hooks and lines to dry out my wet gear, a picnic table, and an abundant water source. I did my laundry in the creek and ate butter and herb noodles for supper. I called my wife and caught up a little before my cell phone died for lack of a battery charge.

Carlisle, Pennsylvania

Walking the Pennsylvania pasture lands the next day, I skirted Carlisle (Russ and Nick's home). It was a farming community with large homes often coupled with barns a hundred yards either behind or beside the century-old wood-framed houses.

The trail cut along the fence lines of the farms and the edge of the tree line. It was a worn footpath cutting through lush pastures. Large tracts of plowed ground with rock-size clods were everywhere. It was a community that lived close to the land.

Along the way that day, I met *Teva Foot* from Alaska and *Me and You* from Massachusetts. I spent the night alone at Cove Mountain Shelter.

Every day the trail had surprises from the people who told of their adventures to the unexpected wildlife encounters from bird and beast. Yes, there were times that I would walk for miles without coming across man or beast, yet the sounds of the wilderness were still in the air.

Wednesday morning was a wonderful time walking the meadowlands, but by the afternoon I was battling boulders and bugs. My feet were tender after eight days on the trail, especially taking on the notorious Pennsylvania boot-breaking rocks.

As I added the miles, a cloud of gnats circled my head. They were like terrorists specializing in torment, provoking me all afternoon. I complained. I sent them to hell. I prayed for grace. I asked what good were they for? A friend once reminded me that one of the titles for Satan in the Scripture was Beelzebub, which meant "lord of the flies."

Flies may feed the songbirds, but they took away my song. Even when I made it to the shelter, they pestered me at the waterhole. They loved the "meat" of the ears. Like Cheyenne Indians, they landed, did a coup, and flew off. The more I swatted, the worse they got, and the worse my attitude was to boot. They buzzed around me until sunset, and at some point, I moved passed caring what the varmints did.

Duncannon, Pennsylvania

Plans for the next morning were to quickstep four miles into Duncannon for breakfast, then hike up to Peter's Mountain Shelter.

During the night I awoke with a start, hearing a critter moving around below my elevated bunk in the shelter. I found my headlamp and peered into the face of a good-size porcupine. I said, "Scat!" And with my rude insult he was gone. Chew marks were evident everywhere on the edge of the wood construction in the shelter. He scampered off in the woods and I rolled over for a good night's rest.

When the birds greeted the sunrise the next morning, I packed up and pointed my trekking poles to the big town of Duncannon. It was set right on the Susquehanna River. I walked through town under gray clouds and rain, looking for a truck stop I had been told about from the trail news network. I crossed the Clark's Ferry Bridge over the Juniata River, and then took a second bridge over the Susquehanna.

Then, just off highways US 22 and 322, I noted the trail cutting back up the green mountain. I had missed the truck stop somehow, so I doubled back across the second bridge. I asked for directions and was soon sitting down in the diner.

I leaned my backpack and poles in the corner of a booth and ate a hearty country breakfast: pancakes, sausage, biscuits, bacon, eggs over-well, grapefruit juice, and a big glass of water. It tasted great to my palate, but on the other side of a divider a trucker wasn't so happy. He told the waitress to never put hot eggs on a cold plate. The manager was called.

After they left, I told the trucker, "When you've been out in the back-woods anything tastes good."

He nodded. When I got up and hoisted my backpack, he said, "You really mean it, don't you?"

Before returning to the trail, I re-supplied in the truck stop store. I walked out with curious eyes staring after me. On the way back across the second bridge, the temperamental trucker gave me a big blast on his horn and waved. I had made a friend.

It was a sixteen-mile day. I saw *Mid-Life Crisis* from Wisconsin on the trail. *Dr. D, Torch*, and *Zen Monkey* were in the shelter that final night of the hike. Arrival time was about 4 P.M. *Zen Monkey* and I caught up for an hour or so before *Dr. D* and *Torch* came into the shelter. The water supply was exactly 370 steps down the mountain (I counted them), then back up again.

The other men came in during a thunderstorm. There was an old shelter about fifty yards away. A lightning bolt had hit and the two men had ditched their poles and packs to run for cover in the old shelter. When things calmed down, they discovered the much more modern shelter we were in nearby.

There we were in the middle of the wilderness: *Zen Monkey*, an emergency room doctor, and the other two men, professors with their doctorates. All four of us were living out of our backpacks, chasing after our dream of conquering a few mountain miles—all with advanced degrees.

Clark's Valley

When dawn broke, I took to the trail. I hiked just seven miles to PA 325 at Clark's Valley. *Zen Monkey* caught up with me at the road and made a few adjustments to his pack, which had sprung a leak from his water platypus. It was a little sad leaving him after bumping into each other so often.

While we waited for my shuttle ride, the gnats moved in for the kill. I looked back on the morning with gratitude because I had taken a bad fall on a slick rock. It could have resulted in a broken arm or injured leg instead of just a case of bruised pride. It had been my first fall in ten days.

It was 10 A.M., and the adventure was over for now, having traveled the highlands of Virginia, West Virginia, Maryland and Pennsylvania. I was ready to let my feet rest and get back to being a pastor to my people and a family man.

Living in the wilderness was wonderful. I always came back to town with a clear head, a clean heart, a fit physique, and lots of stories. For now, the adventures would have to wait until the next season came along, and that was sure to add to the tales of the trail.

He putteth forth his hand upon the rock; he overturneth the mountains by the roots. He cutteth out rivers among the rocks; and his eye seeth every precious thing. (Job 28:9-10)

ROMANCE AND REALITY

There is a romance to the trail. It is akin to cowboy legends, mountain men among the Indians, and action films in the grand outdoors. The wilderness promises adventure, toughness, and peak experiences with your face to the sunset while deer herds cross the skyline.

But reality is quite different. You can go from boldness and daring to blisters and delirium. Your adventure may be uphill to pain and a little agony, and back downhill to very real human restraints that pop the make-believe bubble of silly dreams.

You can buy the gear, shop for the backpacking trends online, and even train and prepare your body with a stair-stepper, but there's nothing like hitting the trail to test a man's resolve. Backpacking magazine looks great, yet real backpacking is not recorded on surreal glossy colored pages.

Hardship reveals much about what's really inside a person. Very often we discover some ladies can out-hike men, and some unlikely candidates just keep on going and going, and do not know what it means to quit. What the trail brings out in people will surprise you.

In the autumn of the tenth year of hiking the highland footpath, we measured the distance between backpacking romance and backcountry reality. Here's the story: *Prune Picker* had recruited and trained two younger men. We were the old men of our troop at forty-four years old.

The other men were twenty-two and thirty-nine. One would be our culinary specialist and had a heart as big as the Pocono Mountains of Pennsylvania. His name was *Rim Runner*. The youngest in age was *Carolina Folly*. He had spent time in the Army and was built lean and mean.

Our seven-day-hike was cut short by torrential rains. We went ninety-two miles altogether. We had enough food for twenty-one days. That became a real factor in what transpired in those late days of October. I had learned in the early years that weight was an enemy, but these guys were not that experienced.

I flew into Allentown, and the men picked me up in a late model SUV. That night we divided the abundant food supply evenly and loaded our gear into bulging backpacks. After a night's rest in the motel, we arranged to meet *Junker* (Robert Freeman) so he could get us to the trailhead early.

Our highland adventure started in the gravel parking lot at Clark's Valley on PA 325, near a footbridge that led north to a series of wilderness challenges that awaited all of us. It was twelve miles later that we laid our trekking poles up against Rausch Gap Shelter. As usual, I was a bit ambitious for the first day out.

One note in my Data Book from the day recalls a story from the region about Mary Jamison. Her nickname was "White Squaw". She had been captured by Indians at the age of fifteen. She married two chiefs and died at age ninety. Such stories have always fascinated me, especially pages from the folklore of the wilderness.

It had been a day of clear blue skies with a few fall colors. We walked across laughing brooks as we chased the mountain trail. We should have broken in a little easier, but Rausch Gap was the first shelter we came to and none of us had prepared for tent camping.

Blister Free

The next day we met *Blister Free* from Rhode Island, traveling south. He was hiking in tennis shoes. He went light and never had any blisters. He had hiked the Pacific Crest Trail (2,700 miles) from Washington State to Oregon and all the way down through California.

His given name was Brett Tucker, and he was moving light on his feet when we met him. He stopped for a few moments to tell us about himself. We were immediately struck by his sparse gear and good attitude. He moved through the woods like he was out for a mile hike rather than a couple of thousand.

He was a rare hiker without any foot troubles. I e-mailed him after I returned home. A few months later I received a reply. Brett was a writer and adventurer. He had finished the Appalachian Trail. He let me in on a few of his secrets for packing light and saving the feet from blisters:

1. Start big and work toward minutia. No need to cut your toothbrush in half. He recommended GoLite gear. For example, their Breeze Pack weighed less than a pound empty.

2. A base weight load of ten to twelve pounds was what he suggested. Blister Free said you could go light without sacrificing comfort by focusing on needs over wants.

3. Everyone can benefit by taking a critical look at equipment choices. Here was his often quoted axiom: "The more you carry the more you'll enjoy the camping. The less you carry the more you'll enjoy the hiking."

Tucker said the best book on lightweight hiking was Ray Jardine's *Beyond Backpacking*, in which he served as an editor. He noted two websites for reference: www.golite.com and www.rayjardine.com.

Blister Free signed off his e-mail: "Happy Trails, Mate." When we met on the trail, he thought I was from Australia. My accent is a quick version of an Arkansas-Oklahoma-Texas mix. He was a rare breed, a backpacker with skill and finesse. Many of the trekkers I knew had not mastered the craft of weight and comfort on the long stretches of the trail, including myself.

We had crossed paths in the rugged miles of rocky Pennsylvania. It would have been so much better to have met him in the first few miles of Georgia. What a contrast he was to the troop he came upon that October day. He was light on his feet, and we were overloaded. His unconventional way of hiking made good sense. Simple is always better. After all, backpackers are out there to enjoy the hike, not punish themselves.

Unfortunately, far too often too many long-distance hikers, in their zeal to be fully equipped, buy too much gear with too much weight all for too much pain in the pocketbook, the back, and the feet. In fact, there was no less than a thousand dollars-worth of new and heavy equipment on the backs of two of our troop of four. As I put my nose to the north, *Blister Free*'s counsel inspired me not to carry the weight of the world on my shoulders.

Pine Grove Shelter

A bit too gung-ho again, I led the men on a seventeen-mile day. They didn't want me to hold back. Still it was not wise to go at my pace, and it would prove detrimental in the days to come. Pine Grove Shelter, right on PA 501, was enclosed. It was all the better since it was a wet night. We cooked turkey and vegetables on a tin table top inside.

The water source was a nearby spigot on the side of the caretaker's house. The bunkhouse setup was much warmer than the open-air trail shelters, so we slept well and got out early with rain falling from gray skies. Two or three other hikers had joined us for the night.

Eagle's Nest Shelter was our next stopover. It was fifteen miles away.

We saw fourteen Mennonite school children and three thru-hikers, including *KOOP* (Keep on One Path) from Livonia, Michigan. *Carolina Folly* had a rough day. His feet were tender. He hurt everywhere.

We slowed down for him, but he decided to pull out when we got to PA 183, nine miles into the day's hike. We flagged down a truck and he got a ride into Hamburg. Our youngest partner had found the trail unbearable and the condition deplorable. It had been zero joy for him, so he took the rest of the week off in a motel room.

That night the three of us had beef and gravy, potatoes, and corn. *Rim Runner* called these meals "one pan wonders." He had brought drink mixes, puddings, and even pancakes for trail meals. Our new friend, *KOOP*, also shared tapioca pudding with us. While we filled up on the tasty meal, the rains kept coming. The winds howled. It got cold.

Our esteemed cook was beat-up too. He said he had "the heart but not the body." His feet were covered in blisters, and he was in a lot of pain. He decided to pull off when we came into Port Clinton the next day. *Rim Runner* had sent a food drop there to the post office.

Port Clinton, Pennsylvania

The three of us walked nine miles into the railroad town not far from Reading, Pennsylvania. The first sight we took in was an old engine and a line of restored railroad cars on the tracks. The train excited *Prune Picker*. It was a train lover's paradise set-up to recall the heydays of shipping coal by the rail.

When we crossed the tracks into the town proper, we found an outdoor center and the post office where a large box of food awaited us. I hoisted it in wonder—what a huge load of grub!

We hitched a ride into nearby Hamburg. It was a real spectacle seeing three backpacks, a large parcel, and three unshaved backwoodsmen riding in the back of a little red pickup truck. We all piled in and held on for our lives.

Carolina Folly had set up his living quarters in a nice Microtel Inn on Rt. 61 and I-78, right across from Cabela's Outdoor Center. We had a hot shower and shave before taking in the store. A fellow could go loco in there, where every imaginable thing was for sale.

They had elaborate wildlife displays with bear, trophy deer, mountain lions, and even an arctic wilderness display. It was a man's amusement park. Upstairs was a restaurant where we had lunch. It was superb: barbeque brisket, home fries, and apple dumplings.

Eric had one of his trekking poles repaired. I managed to make it out of there without spending anything but lunch money. That took some real discipline, besides the fact that I could not carry the weight.

We got our laundry done, repacked, called family, and I checked on the church back home where I was pastor. While the younger guys had called it quits, *Prune Picker* and I were preparing for a few more days up in the highlands.*Rim Runner* planned to visit his brother in Rhode Island whom he had not seen in quite a while. *Carolina Folly* would camp out at the motel, playing video games and watching movies. We would all come back together at the beginning of the next week.

When the sun rose the next morning, *Prune Picker* and I climbed out of Port Clinton to the heights above. One of the motel employees gave us a ride to the trail. This was one of the best days on the trail. The colors were pristine. We had blue skies and cotton-ball clouds.

It was day eighty-five for me on the Appalachian Trail. We went past Pulpit Rock and Pinnacle, and added another fifteen miles to our boots. We rolled out our thermo-rests and sleeping bags at Eckville Shelter, right on Hawk Mountain Road. We had it to ourselves for the first few hours.

There were thirty thousand birds of prey in that part of the state, fourteen different species. We spotted a lot of them along the ridgelines as we walked on the edge of the woods and cliffs. We also heard a couple of stories from that part of the northern Appalachians.

Delaware Indian Tales

In 1737, the white pioneers and the Indians agreed to what was called a "Walking Purchase." However far the white men could walk in a given day would become their possession. The Indians knew they could walk and hunt twenty-to-thirty miles a day. That is what they expected to give to the white man. But the white men took their "walk" that day at a "dead run" and covered sixty-one and one-fourth miles. Needless to say, the Indians were not happy neighbors.

Here's the second story: In December 1763, fifty Scotch-Irish men called the "Paxton Boys" killed six Delaware Indian women, an old man, and child. Thirteen Indians escaped and were jailed for their own safety—so they were told. Then one hundred men linked to the Paxtons killed them in cold blood.

It was called the Conestoga Massacre. When the terror was over, a total of six old men, six women, six boys, and three girls were murdered. At the time, the British government paid 150 dollars for a Delaware scalp.

We had lunch on that wonderful day at the Pinnacle, where we met a couple of ladies who were day-hiking. They shared their food with us. The afternoon was just as good as the morning, so I spent the day praising God in my spirit.

For a little while, we stopped at a fallen tree and dug in around it, imagining what history was buried under its roots. We passed the twelve-hundred mile-marker for the Appalachian Trail. The sun was warm on our faces.

It all made for an unbeatable day, worth the entire trip just to experience it. *Prune Picker* and I cherished our time to share and take on that stretch of wilderness—much of it on top of the world, as we looked down upon valleys and farms far below.

Eckville Shelter

Eckville Shelter was very unusual because it was set right on a paved highway. It was a small cabin behind a house. A washhouse was nearby with all the amenities. The water source was on the back porch of the house, where the caretaker lived.

We came in early, unpacked our gear, had a hearty supper, and began to unwind as the darkness fell. Just when we were about to close our eyes in the bunks we had chosen on opposite walls, we heard voices and saw flashlights cutting the night sky outside.

A Boy Scout troop invaded the place. Two men and twelve boys came banging into the quiet haven. Their gear went flying everywhere while we made room for them. The scout masters took off for a half-an-hour to park their vehicles while we were left to manage the young lads.

The next morning, we ate breakfast, and the scout leaders fixed a man-size buffet for their charges. We exchanged basic introductions, since they had come in after hours the night before, then we bid them farewell.

What a day on the trail that Saturday was for us. It was so busy we could have used traffic signs. There were no less than thirty-nine hikers in the morning and seventy-five in the afternoon. If we added four section hikers in the shelter that night and over fifty tent campers, that accounted for almost 170 people on the trail that day.

Along the way, we had met *Papa Roach* from Maine, to name just one among the many. We crossed the summit of Blue Mountain, traveled past the Cliffs and Bear Rocks, and then came into Bake Oven Knob.

We camped in the shelter on top. I shared it with Andy, Barry, Bob and Steve. *Prune Picker* pulled aside, rolled his sleeping bag out in a little clearing to get some privacy, and talked to his wife on his cell phone.

I slept beside a Jewish gentleman who snored. My earplugs helped a little. When morning came, we got breakfast on our own. Then, *Prune Picker* and I hit the trail under cloudy skies.

It was Sunday morning, and we hoped to find a church in Palmerton. We made it down the mountain to Lehigh River Bridge by mid-morning in quick time. As we descended into the parking lot by the road, we saw it overflowing with vehicles and day-hikers.

We had every intention of returning to the trail, but wet weather would keep us in town. We knew if we committed to going farther north, it would be twenty miles before we would hit another paved road where the guys could find us.

Palmerton, Pennsylvania

We hitched a ride into town with a family who had a young son. The car was a small hatchback full of all kinds of odds and ends. We somehow squeezed everything into the compact car. They took us to the police station, where an officer put us up in the town's hostel provided for long-distance hikers.

The living quarters were in the basement of a city building where the Boy Scouts had built bunks for backpackers. We had it to ourselves. After getting our gear in order and taking a quick rinse, we crossed the town square and went to the Living Hope Lighthouse for Sunday morning church service.

They were a young congregation with a small band of believers, who met in an old traditional facility. The teaching was solid and faithful to the Scripture and the worship songs were contemporary. The only thing lacking was friendliness.

We walked down the main street to a German pizza place called Palmerton's Pizza. It was on the corner of a town block, just across from a recreational field where little fellows were playing football as their families watched on the sidelines.

We returned to our basement bunkhouse for a shower, to clean up our gear, and debate about going back on the trail. Both of us wanted to, but the question was over the soggy weather.

I had chicken and broccoli noodles for supper on the backpacking stove. Eric and I had a prayer time and did some heart-to-heart talking.

There we were, having known each other in our early twenties and now back out on a second trek as family men in our mid-forties. We spoke of what the Lord was teaching us through our family life, Christian service, and our reading. For the most part, our kinship was the love of the same things in life, starting with our love for God.

Yes, it had been a good day. Though it was cloudy and a little wet, the autumn colors were still evident.

On Monday morning we woke up at six. Eric went for coffee and a paper. We ate breakfast later at Bert's. I had a farmer's omelet and blueberry pancakes—all under five dollars.

We spent the rest of the morning reading from the little library the city had assembled at the hostel and then packed up. For that time and season, we had hiked our last mile on the trail. The weather prevented us from hiking on in the vegetation barren wilderness in the miles leading north. We decided to join our other two partners and take in some sights.

Annapolis, Maryland

Our partners picked us up in a downpour of rain before lunch. We drove to Annapolis to see the Navy Academy and then took in Gettysburg. We made our way to the airport, where the men returned to California and I flew south back to my home in Tennessee.

In retrospect, *Rim Runner* said he learned he did not come to Pennsylvania to hike—that was not his real purpose. After hearing him tell about his meeting with his brother, we had to agree. It had been a divine appointment. The family had been alienated and his visit reunited brother to brother, and later, his brother to his mother as well.

Tidbits from the Trail

Every section of the Appalachian Trail provided fresh stories that my people back home loved to hear sprinkled into sermons. A few tidbits I heard from the trail that autumn included a bear story in the setting of the Great Smoky Mountains.

The varmint had learned to come up behind a backpacker and tug on his backpack. The typical hiker would abandon it from fright. The bear would then chow down on the foodstuffs he found. It makes you wonder who was the smarter of the creatures.

Another story told of an Indian hiker, who left his pack on a mountain trail with a note attached inviting those who passed by to take whatever they wanted with one caution: a rattler was attached to the pack to keep everyone honest. Sometimes on the trail, it was hard to tell which of the stories were folklore, and which were real life chronicles.

There is a lot of romance to the trail from a distance; but close up, the hard realities separate one adventurer from another. There were plenty of surprises when trekking the tough terrain of the high country of Pennsylvania. The truth is, the trail says much more about us than we can say about it.

God thundereth marvelously with his voice; great things doth he, which we cannot comprehend. For he saith to the snow, Be thou on the earth; likewise to the small rain, and to the great rain of his strength. (Job 37:5-6)

HIGH ADVENTURE IN
NEW ENGLAND

Accessing the Appalachian Trail became a bi-annual commitment in the last several years of reaching for Mount Katahdin. The next spring, I returned to Palmerton, Pennsylvania, went northbound on the trail again, and spent fifteen days taking in experiences I would never forget.

Over a lifetime, I have lived in 10 American states, and though Arkansas was home as far as my family and youth, at times no place felt more like home than the wilderness. It was there that my soul was at rest, and every experience in the highlands became a treasure to remember.

In those two weeks and one day, I crossed Delaware Water Gap on the Pennsylvania-New Jersey state line, enjoyed the hospitality of small town Unionville, New York, took in the walk-thru zoo at Bear Mountain, reveled in the beautiful climbs of Connecticut, and got off the trail at one of the road crossings for the Housatonic River.

It was a 231-mile trip through New England on foot and pure pleasure, except for the first night.

The more I walked those mountain trails, the more joys and adventures seemed to intensify. Every day brought some new turn in the trail that made me marvel at the unmistakable hand of God. I saw his hand in the wonders of the wood and the magnanimity of the mountains I climbed. Even the people I met revealed the creative genius of God in looks, personality and conversation.

Spring made my adrenalin rush as I anticipated returning to the trail. I made the connection flying from Nashville, Tennessee, to Allentown, Pennsylvania. There wasn't much sleep the night before the trip as I struggled with packing too much gear. I knew I would have it down to a science about the time I reached Katahdin.

The first day back out was without question the toughest. Janet Goloub, President of the Allentown Hiking Club, was very gracious to give me a ride from the Fairfield Inn to the trailhead.

What a hike it was! The little climb out of Palmerton led to a ten-mile stretch where the land had little vegetation due to zinc poisoning. I crossed a road at the five-mile marker and another at a little over twelve miles. That would have been a good place to call it a day, but there was no shelter.

When All the Alarms went Off

The Leroy A. Smith Shelter was sixteen miles up the trail, a hard first day. I met *Wriven* (Celtic for "dragon") early in the day, but no one else until I came to the shelter at 3 P.M.

There, a nameless hunter already occupied the shelter. When I walked up and dropped my pack, all my alarms went off. When you're by yourself for hours in the wilderness, you gain a sixth sense about people you meet. I didn't feel good about this guy.

He was in his late twenties, short and a little stocky. As soon as I started to engage him in conversation, he not only ignored me, but he rolled down his pants legs and started putting on layers of clothing though it was a mild autumn day.

I noted a hatchet on a table and a high-powered rifle hanging over his head in the shelter. After he put two coats on, he took the rifle off the hook, and then disappeared into the woods. All the time I was praying "Lord, do

I stay or do I go?" I received clear direction to move on. I filled my water bottles and vamoosed.

Wind Gap, Pennsylvania

Hiking seven miles after leaving the unpredictable character in the Smith Shelter, I came into Wind Gap. Along the way I warned a couple of teenage girls traveling southbound on the trail about my earlier encounter.

The trail had been rocky, my feet were blistered, and I was beat-up after twenty-three miles. Walking over a mile on PA 33, I found a Travel Inn Motel for the night.

The next morning, the son of the Asian Indian proprietor gave me a ride back to the trail on his commute to college classes. It had rained overnight. The night's rest had given a little relief to my feet. I was on the trail by 8:10 A.M. Backpacking past Wolf Rocks, over Mount Minsi, then around Lookout Rock and Council Rock, I came down a gradual drop into Delaware Water Gap.

Delaware Water Gap, Pennsylvania

It was 3:30 P.M. The church hostel in town where I had hoped to stay was getting some renovation. I met Brian Hill, a state bridge supervisor, who gave me a ride to the Ramada Inn. He was a backpacker, bicyclist and avid outdoorsman. When I inquire about his faith, he told me he was a "shouting Methodist."

Supper was at a local cafe where I ordered a Greek salad and spinach pie. That night I called Prune Picker to let him know how it was going. I was a little footsore and sunburned, but no complaints. I had only spotted three hikers on that windy and cloudy day, but there was no rain.

I checked out of the Ramada Inn by 9 A.M., catching a ride with Evelyn, a housekeeper at the motel. It would be a short day of only ten miles, crossing into New Jersey, the eighth state for north bounders. The trail was still very rocky, but the bald tops had some wonderful views, which made the tough miles worthwhile.

Mohican Outdoor Center

My water was about gone by 2:30 P.M., when I came into the Mohican Outdoor Center, a hostel located on a gravel road. I only encountered three day hikers on the trail and had the Outdoor Center bunkhouse to myself that night. Dave was the caretaker and he was very helpful. I filed a report with him on the character I had seen at Leroy A. Smith Shelter two nights before.

After a hot shower, I fixed supper: mixed vegetables and an apple cider packet. I spent some time reading about the hut system in New Hampshire from information lying around the center, and did some planning for the fall hike. As the day ended, I could hear the crickets out in the woodland and the frogs singing in the pond out back.

It was the fourth night away from home. Three nights had been in motels and one in the Outdoor Center. Most long-distance backpackers take their nights in the woods, except for once every week to ten days when they go into town to clean up and re-supply. Some stay two or three weeks before they come off the trail. My more frequent town stops were due to my dependence on shelters. They were not always available when I needed one because I tended to hike a few more miles rather than stop at a shelter mid-afternoon.

I read the Bible and prayed, then closed my eyes in the quiet bunkhouse for a great night's rest.

As I rolled over and opened my eyes to a new day, I heard rain falling outside. It was 5:30 A.M. I got a quick rinse in the sink, fixed oatmeal in the kitchen, and had devotions before hitting the trail by 7 A.M.

On that day, I went up Rattlesnake Mountain. Fortunately, I did not meet the namesake of the mountain. I introduced myself to a couple that was section-hiking. Their home was right there in New Jersey. It was 4:30 P.M. when I unlaced my boots. Ahhh. Isaiah, a thru-hiker from Maine, was going south on the trail. He had come in just before I did. He was twenty-four years old and on the quiet side. He was in his bedroll by 7 P.M., fast asleep.

Supper was always a treat: I had alfredo noodles. When darkness fell on the wilderness, I was sleeping there in the open air at Gren Anderson Shelter, a twenty-one-mile trek from the Mohican Outdoor Center.

Morning broke, and I had the trail all to myself for twenty miles. The views had been great along the trail. I spotted a turkey on the ground as well as a turtle and a Canadian goose by a pond. It was Saturday, and I was hoping for a place to stay in town so that I could take in church on Sunday.

Unionville, New York

Walking into Unionville, New York, I followed an old railroad bed. When I hit the residential area, I started scouting for churches, a good place for information and direction. The First Presbyterian Church was right on Main Street. People were milling around the stairs and foyer for an event of some kind.

Stepping into the entrance of the church, I took off my backpack and set my poles behind a stairway. There was no hostel or lodging in town, but the church was having a spaghetti supper. The church members invited me to stay. They said they would also call the police department and arrange for me to camp out in the city park gazebo.

When I went to the church-dining hall, people were very open and friendly to this southern stranger. I took a seat across from Fred and Holly Heinzmann and their boys, Erich and Paul. On my plate were the biggest meatballs I had ever seen (worthy of an eighty-mile hike), spaghetti sauce, French bread, a salad side dish, and a chocolate brownie.

Holly had been on the trail down south in previous years and Fred had done some long- distance kayaking up north. They asked me a few questions, and then invited me to their home for a shower. They ended up doing my laundry, encouraged me to call my family, and let me roll my sleeping bag out on their front porch.

At ten o'clock that evening, I was writing a few notes in my journal with a heart full of rejoicing at all the kindness of this family. The next morning, we had a hearty breakfast, and I joined the Heinzmanns for Sunday School, church, and a spaghetti lunch for the whole church. Leftovers! I loaded up on those meatballs all over again.

Pastor Robert Keene was a gracious man who loved his people. He kept them smiling that morning with visual illustrations during his sermon. He was animated and easily held their attention.

That afternoon, I walked the Wallkill River Road and went over Pochuck Mountain, going just eight miles before I came out on County Road 565 into Glenwood, New Jersey. It was late in the day, and there was no shelter for another nine miles, so I looked for an inexpensive place for overnight.

Glenwood, New Jersey

Hiking past Glenwood Baptist Church, I decided to knock on the house next door, which I thought might be the manse for the church. It was. Bob and Beverly Ingraham were home and pointed me down the road to a bed and breakfast. I thanked them and kept walking.

Bob said that when I left, he thought, "What am I doing?" He tracked me down in his car and brought me back to the house.

Once again, a family opened up their home. There, I got a bath, supper (great leftovers), and had some sweet fellowship around the table.

Then I camped out in the church, where I called my in-laws, wife, and a lady in our church that had experienced a tragedy. My feet were still tender, but it was good to be in a dry and warm place for the night. I had a good prayer time at the church altar and ended up sleeping on the pews for a little cushion.

On Monday morning, one of the ladies from the church gave me a ride back to the trail. It was a wet day. In fact, I got soaked and dried out four different times during the next twenty-one miles.

Warwick, New Jersey

I came out at Vernon on New Jersey 94. Ed, a Jewish psychologist picked me up on the road. He had just finished a five-day-hike himself. We went into Warwick, had lunch at a pizza place (I had pineapple pizza), picked up supplies at Eckerd's, and then Ed took me back to the trail.

At Wawayanda Shelter, I saw a thru-hiker named *Cowboy*, but no one else on the trail all day. It was a hard day fighting boulders, a deluge of rain, and water on the trail. I hate to admit it, but I worked hard to keep myself from cussing the Appalachian Trail planners who put the trail straight across the top of boulders and slick inclines. They must have mapped it out on a day of sunshine. I did repent of my murmurings and found some joy in the rainy torrent.

Greenwood Lake, New York

I hit the pavement at New York 17A, and then hoofed it on in to the little hamlet of Greenwood Lake, where I scouted up and down one end of town for an affordable place to stay. I ate at a diner and made some calls from there. A taxi driver picked me up and took me to the Breezy Inn for the night.

When I opened the door to the little motel room the next morning, I looked out to a lake full of sunshine. The same taxi driver picked me up to take me to catch breakfast at the diner, and then he drove me two more miles to the trail crossing. It was a late start, but at least my feet would get a little reprieve before trekking sixteen miles to Fingerboard Shelter.

That day was everything the previous day had not been. It was beautiful. I did do combat with flies, gnats, and a hoard of insects. I was on the trail by 9:30 A.M. and hiked until 7 P.M.

I went through the Lemon Squeezer, where I had to hoist my pack and poles up to the next level in a tight rock climb. As far as wear and tear on the body, my shins hurt a little, but the feet were much better. I finally resorted to a knit cap to keep the bugs away from my ears.

Cowboy joined me in the shelter around 7:30 P.M. He and I would bump into each other off and on for the next few days. For example, the next day we arrived at Bear Mountain about the same time, and marveled at the New York City skyline some thirty-four miles away.

Fort Montgomery, New York

Day ninety-six on the Appalachian Trail was one to remember. I felt like I was part of the trail culture after eight days. There were three mountains and a zoo on the path leading to Ft. Montgomery, New York, where I stopped that night.

After taking on Goshen, Black, and Bear Mountains, cutting across five roads and an interstate, I descended upon Bear Mountain Inn Resort and inquired about lodging. They were booked up and doing a lot of remodeling. It was an ideal setting with a walking track that wrapped around behind the Inn by a lake and a picturesque green surrounding mammoth-size accommodations.

The desk clerk was super, and she made a few calls to see what else was available. She reserved a room at Bear Mountain Bridge Motel with owner Doug Johnson. I had only walked fourteen miles, but I was ready to put my feet up.

Just past the Bear Mountain Inn Resort, the trail led right through a little zoo, where I saw my second black bear on the Appalachian Trail. I tried to strike up a conversation with the varmint, but he was disinterested (probably an agnostic). Along the path through the zoo, there were soft drink and food vending machines (I got an ice cream).

Coming out of the zoo, I found myself in traffic crossing the Bear Mountain Bridge. At that point, I wasn't sure which side of the lake the motel was on, so I went to the other side and doubled back. Doug pulled up looking for me. He took care of hikers all the time.

He told me some memorable stories from his many years' experience with hikers, especially thru-hikers.

He shook his head and said, "Sometimes these guys spend so long in the woods, it takes us three days to air out the room when they leave."

His motel was very hiker-friendly.

At the Bear Mountain Bridge Motel, I took a hot shower and shaved off my two-month old beard. I did my laundry and hung it out on the bushes outside, cleaned up my pack, and called my sweetheart. Then I limped into town for a chef salad at a deli, where I also restocked. There I bought a package of white chocolate pretzels and a peach Snapple for an evening snack.

When I walked out of the deli in the little town, I spotted *Cowboy* for the last time. I crossed the traffic and we traded stories of the last day or so. He was camping in his tent in a spot overlooking the road lined with a row of homes and businesses. He had to wait there for a post office drop of supplies.

Doug gave me a ride to the bridge the following morning, and I started to climb again on one of the last days of April. On the trail by 8 A.M., I hiked until 6 P.M., for an eighteen-mile day.

Only two hikers were going southbound that day. One was a section-hiker called *Anchor*, the other was a "flip-flopper" named Mike. A flip-flopper hikes from one end of the trail to the middle, then takes it up on the other end and hikes back to the middle again. It is one way to avoid the extreme temperatures of winter or summer.

Carmel, New York

There was no shelter that day at the eighteen-mile marker, just a road crossing by Canopus Lake near Fahnestock State Park. The next shelter was seven miles north, so I sat my pack and poles on the shoulder of the road not far from Carmel, New York (close to West Point), and stuck out my thumb.

I had been praying all day for a place to stay. About twenty minutes later, Jerry from Connecticut stopped. He had been day hiking. Originally from the Czech Republic and a practicing Roman Catholic, he was very kind to his fellow hiker.

We stopped at a ranger's house, and I inquired about staying over-night in a stone pavilion across the road. He gave me permission, and told me about showers at the campground. Jerry took me to the campground, but the showers were dirty and foul, so I passed. He drove me back to the pavilion, and we said goodbye.

Laying my pack by a picnic table, I tried to get a cold drink from one of two vending machines without success. I started up the stairs to the stone pavilion, when a motorist pulled into the gravel parking lot and called out.

Mark Tippett had been an Appalachian Trail section-hiker and was originally from Memphis, Tennessee. He was on his way into town to go to the post office when he had seen me earlier trying to catch a ride. When he returned on his way home, he tracked me down. Asking me where I was going, I told him I was camping out in the pavilion.

He said, "There are too many mice in there. Come on home with me."

As the sun died on the horizon, I was awestruck at the turn of events. Mark took me to his house, gave me a bedroom, and let me shower. He introduced me to his girlfriend Tildy (Matilda), and Hawthorne (their golden lab), and then spread out supper. He was a painter and carpenter, and she worked for an Environmental Protection Agency in New York.

This Good Samaritan had been an ironman athlete, a graduate of a Bible College, and had been in the youth ministry. He had plans to get a Master's degree in English. We had a great time telling part of our life stories.

They fixed a fantastic salad and pasta meal. Then they insisted that I call my wife on their nickel. What hospitality and what an answer to prayer!

After a good night's rest in a real bed and a bite of breakfast, Tildy prepared a ham and cheese sandwich for lunch on the trail. Mark dropped me off on the road where I had come out the night before.

It was an exceptional day with great views. There were a few mud holes to deal with along the trail, the gnats were buzzing, and I worked up a sweat on the uphills while traveling sixteen miles.

When I came into Morgan Stewart Shelter at 3:30 P.M., Ed Dexter, age sixty-seven, was already there. He was a retired mechanical engineer and a member of First Baptist Church, Knoxville, Tennessee. We lived in the same region of East Tennessee, only to meet in the backcountry of New York State. He had invested a couple of decades going north on the big trail.

We went for the water source downhill and returned to cook supper. Two weekend hikers came in, a couple named Ron and Christy, who were tent camping nearby. They were New Yorkers.

Saturday was a beautiful morning, with the trail cutting beside a lake, along rumbling brooks, through pastures, and up a few mountains. I saw fourteen Boy Scouts, a father and his two sons, two section-hikers from Massachusetts named *Ephraim* and *Quasi*, twenty senior citizens who were part of a hiking club, and two other day-hikers.

Dover Plains, New York

After hiking only eleven miles, I came out on New York Highway 22 to the Appalachian Trail Railroad Station. It was 12:30 P.M. On the roadside was a hotdog stand I had heard about from the trail scuttlebutt. I had a loaded dog and a Diet Coke.

Seheid, an African-American Muslim, had stopped to get a bite to eat as well. We talked and he offered me a ride nine miles into Dover Plains. He was very helpful and dropped me off at the Foothills Motel.

I cleaned up, did laundry, and hung the clothes on the bushes out back. After the backpack was put back in order, I watched a bit of *Braveheart*. When 5:30 P.M. came around, I was ready to take in supper at a little diner and get a few supplies for the days ahead.

Finding a church off the trail on Sundays was always a real challenge, but that is why I had come into town the night before. I went to a convenience store that morning and dropped my pack and poles just inside the door.

Taking in a quick breakfast of sausage, egg, and a cheese muffin with a pint of milk, I spied a nicely dressed African-American gentleman coming my way for his morning brew. I asked him if he was going to church and he smiled in the affirmative. So, I inquired about which church he was attending.

In my reasoning, he was an African American brother, so he was on his way to a black church. We loaded up my pack, and this Baptist deacon and Sunday school teacher drove us to First Baptist Church of Dover. It was a multicultural church with an Italian pastor name Brother Tony Bacino.

The people and pastor were more-than-gracious. We had a good Bible class and spirited service, and then Brother Harold Roberson, my African American brother, took me out for a deli lunch before hitting the trail. I had pork and veggies, a Diet Mountain Dew, and a pastry. Food is always good in town. He had to go on, so I ate it on the roadside.

That afternoon I enjoyed the last few miles of New York, walking through pasturelands, a few sloughs, up a climb or two, and prepared myself for the last few days with a friend. After you walk thirteen days alone there is a little adjustment, but I was looking forward to times of rich fellowship with my pastor friend.

Bruce James was the Pastor of the Gallup Hills Baptist Church in Ledyard, Connecticut. He and I had been friends for over decade. His wife was from the county I ministered to in East Tennessee. They had family in our church. I met him at 4:30 P.M. on Hoyt Road in Wingdale, New York, right by the Connecticut line.

We hiked to the Ten-Mile Lean-To for a total of ten miles that Sunday. It was a great spot not far from the Ten Mile River. We sat in the shelter overlooking a nice pasture, leaned back, and talked until the sun went down and the stars twinkled bright in the night sky. We had it all to ourselves, and it was good.

Monday was a wet day with some tough uphill climbs. Bruce decided his knees couldn't take the steep elevations, so he walked the roads and met me at the end of the day.

Hiking Schaghticoke Mountain along the New York and Connecticut line, moving past Indian Rocks, on to Caleb's Peak, and then down the unforgettable St. Johns Ledges, made for an intense yet spectacular day, even though it was wet. St. Johns Ledges was a rocky, steep, downhill scramble that tested any hiker.

Another highlight that day was finding a little downy owl on the side of the trail. I took a good look, but gave him space. Calling out with my best hoot owl cry, I located the mother about fifty yards away up in a tree branch. I just wanted to be sure she knew where her little one was.

Two miles before I came into another shelter, Bruce had tied a note and a Payday candy bar to a tree so that I would see it. What a friend! That was a sure sign for encouragement, knowing the end of the trail was near that day. The rest of the way was on a gravel road. I met a ranger and spoke briefly, then taking the trail beside a river walk, I met up with Bruce, and we came to the campsite for the night.

Meeting *Gray Panter*

During the trek, I only saw a single day-hiker, but we met *Gray Panter* in the shelter that afternoon. His trail name was the alias for Ken Stone, who would become a great friend and incredible help in the miles ahead.

He started out as a thru-hiker and ended up hiking the trail in four sections. His home was western Vermont. He was a retired civil engineer and spent his days in the winter teaching snowboarding at Smuggler's Notch, not far from Stowe, Vermont.

We found Ken about mid-afternoon wrapped up in his sleeping bag fast asleep. He woke up and engaged us in conversation as the rains continued to fall outside. The place was called Stewart Hollow Brook Lean-to. It had been a wet sixteen-mile day, but still worthwhile for the good company and the quiet wilderness walk.

Not far from the Housatonic River, the little shelter was home that night. It was the only dry spot in the forest; all the while the rain pelted the tin roof. The night air was cool as we fixed supper (chicken fettuccini). Sleep was sweet, as we hunkered down in the warm sleeping bags and the world all around us got drenched.

It was the last day on the trail. We started right at 7 A.M. Bruce and I walked about two miles along the river. When the trail went up the mountain, he took the river road with the plan to meet me at a road crossing (US 7 and Connecticut 112).

I had a harrowing experience crossing a log to rejoin the trail. The little river I was crossing had swollen with all the rain, and the usual crossing was just too dangerous.

So, I went upriver to a fallen log and made my way halfway across it. When my backpack weight shifted and my hiking poles got in the way, I went to my knees. The old hemlock was slick and water was moving fast beneath me. I held on for dear life and managed to crawl across in between the tines of the fallen tree. Once safe on the other side, I sighed in relief and got back on the trail.

I came to a road and saw *Gray Panter* searching for the trail. He had walked around the crossing about a half-mile and was now seeking to find the trail again. We hiked together until lunch, and then I had to do double-time so I could get to the road to meet Bruce.

It was a beautiful day with green buds everywhere in the forests, blue skies dotted by white clouds, and plenty of rumbling brooks. There were no other hikers but *Gray Panter*. I spotted snakes, songbirds, deer, and chipmunks. I rendezvoused with Bruce at 3 P.M.

We drove back through the towns we had hiked around on Highway 7. It was picturesque New England: little shops, red barns, waterfalls, and churches with tall steeples. He took me to Danbury to pick up a white Ford Focus rental car. Then we had a Chinese buffet in town.

After our goodbyes, I drove down to Allentown, Pennsylvania, where I had started, driving through Connecticut, New York, New Jersey, and back into Pennsylvania.

I spent the night at the same motel I had stayed at two weeks before. The clerk remembered me, and a few men in the lobby asked me about my trail experiences.

The morning after, I had a good breakfast and counted my cash reserve. It was $5.63. I left by noon and flew to Chicago. At the O'Hare Airport I snacked on nuts and pretzels, and drank a Peach Snapple. That was uptown for a man that spent a few days on the trail.

I managed to get the flight bumped up five hours. On that last leg between Chicago and Nashville, I sat beside a Christian counselor, Leslie Vernick, on her way to visit and minister in a Cambodian orphanage.

All the food and company were rich compared to the simple things and long quiet hours in the wild. It felt good. Just walking through New England towns and the countryside was an adventure in itself—besides all the people that I had met and could never forget.

Those sixteen days slimmed me down (I usually lost ten to fifteen pounds on every long-distance hike), made me feel alive, and brought an array of color to my black and white world.

My heart was torn. Yes, I sorely missed my family and my people back in East Tennessee, but there was something about the wilderness and taking the long journey that made life rich without the money, free without the to-do lists, and at peace without the aggravations of the tick-tock of the clock.

THE BEST OF BOTH WORLDS

It was early October, and it was time to do some climbing in New England. *Prune Picker* came in early and scouted out the back roads of Vermont with his sweetheart, taking in the famous hamlet of Stowe. She flew back home to California, and I joined him to pick up the trail for eight days of hiking town-to-town.

We had the best of both worlds. New England towns are like another world to two westerners. The hills and little mountains of Connecticut, Massachusetts, and Vermont waited for us like unopened gifts of intrigue.

Times with my old California soul mate were always warm-hearted. We both cherished the added opportunities to conquer a few peaks, talk about our families, and encourage each other in the Christian faith. No matter how hard the miles were, those times gave my spirit needed refreshment.

Dana Murphy, a trail shuttle driver, helped us make the connection between the motel and the trail. We spoke with him about faith. He was gracious, revealed a little of his background, but he had only a margin of interest. We thanked him and unloaded our pack and poles.

We stretched our legs eleven miles the first day from US 7 on the Housatonic River to Salisbury, Connecticut. Crossing the Mohawk Trail, the Iron Bridge, and Prospect Mountain, we went across US 44 then on to US 41, which led west into Salisbury.

Salisbury, Connecticut

We walked the road into town, just under a mile, and ventured into the Episcopal Church about 3 P.M., where there was a beehive of activity. Prune Picker had a reservation at the White Hart Hotel, but we decided to shop around for a better deal. The ladies at the church pointed us back down US 41, where we came from, to Maria McCabe's.

When we knocked on the door, nobody was home. She soon drove up, and we were introduced to a delightful lady who had originally come from Italy. Upstairs in her green cottage she provided a stopover for hikers for $25 a night, including breakfast.

We had a bite in town late that afternoon from a deli adjacent to a little courtyard, where we also had some coffee and tea from another nearby shop. We came back to the house and sat in the backyard, taking in the final hour of daylight while reading books from Maria's downstairs library.

Mrs. McCabe had been playing cards with her brother-in-law. Once they were finished, she invited us to sit down around the table and enjoy some pumpkin pie. We heard her life story of growing up in Europe and then meeting a service man from the States.

She told us we could get breakfast the next morning on our own. She didn't get up early anymore. We paid her, shared about the things of faith, and she listened. She expressed some misgivings about the church she was raised in as a child.

Maria's story touched two continents, a couple of marriages, and chronicles from eight decades of living and giving out of a generous life. We counted ourselves blessed to have met her.

When we think of her today, we can only smile of a place and time in American life that is quickly fading: an open door, a friendly face, fixing breakfast in a New England lady's kitchen like it was home, and hearing the rich stories of a colorful and remarkable life.

We were ready to go when the sun came up after twelve hours of such marvelous hospitality. *Prune Picker* and I hiked eighteen miles to South Egremont, Massachusetts. It was election year. As we crossed a brook into Massachusetts, we knew we were in a part of the country not friendly toward our political perspectives.

Both of us were constitutionalists and not revisionists. I didn't have as much fun with it as my friend did in the towns along the trail in New England. In that corner of America, the overwhelming flavor was not toward conservative values. Even so, New England hospitality could easily rival most communities down South.

The first day out we had only seen three hikers. The second day was little different. We counted six on the trail, including *Utah Mike* and his dog *Maybe*, as well as *Burch* from Brunswick, Maine. We went to the top of Bear Mountain, around Race Mountain, across Mount Everett, then down to South Egremont on Massachusetts Highway 41.

South Egremont, Massachusetts

The Egremont Inn was built in 1786. We took a spacious room there and rinsed off the day's grime. Walking through town on a breezy autumn evening, we had supper at the Old Mill Restaurant. The most accessible seats in the place were booths near the bar.

It was fine dining for a couple of backpackers. As we ate (I had delicious trout and a salad), we took in the culture all around us. The bar was brimming with local people in a festive mood. That night we watched the vice-presidential debates between John Edwards and Richard Cheney.

Steve, the motel owner, gave us a ride to the trailhead after a restful night. It was 10:15 A.M. when we left—a late start. On the trail again, we met our old friend the Housatonic River. We walked to the top of East Mountain, and along the way introduced ourselves to a couple with a dog named *Hawk* from Delaware, *Bad Start* from New Hampshire, and four men with southern accents.

These Alabama and Georgia boys were gazing down into the wooded valleys when we came upon them. They told us that every year they hiked ten miles of the Appalachian Trail in a different state (there are fourteen in all).

We smiled in admiration. Here were four older men chasing their dream in terms they could accomplish. As a band of brothers, they spurred each other on and explored the ridgelines of the eastern seaboard.

Great Barrington, Massachusetts

Prune Picker and I hit pavement early after just twelve miles. The colors were beginning to change in New England, and we took pleasure in walking under the canopies of leaves. The Data Book indicated there was lodging nearby, but we found out different. It was four miles into town.

A gentleman named Paul Morgan, a local artist and cabinetmaker, loaded us up in his van and showed us the layout of town. He did find the small hostel listed in the Data Book, but it was not near any food sources for our meals. We went to his shop, and he placed a few calls to find lodging. Paul was a skilled watercolor painter. Many of his paintings were of the region and the town of Great Barrington.

Our home for the night was the Day's Inn. We had our end-of-the-day meal at Castle Street Cafe. I had a hamburger. An African-American waitress assisted us, but not before Eric teased another waitress about the Heinz ketchup (made by the company which was owned by Theresa Heinz Kerry, wife of the presidential candidate nominee).

Grinning, he said, "Don't you have any Republican ketchup in here?"
She didn't know how to take him.

The dawn broke in town, and we were waiting at Martins Restaurant when it opened. We had a tasty breakfast and walked to the main highway to catch a ride. A construction crew allowed us to get in the back of their pickup for a mile or two. It was cold.

When they turned off the road to their work site, we hitch-hiked again. Paul Morgan pulled up and opened the van doors. He had been looking for us. What a man! Once we got to the stopping off place, we gave him heartfelt thanks and started climbing.

It had been comparatively easy the day before. The fourth day was our challenge hike: twenty-one miles. There was only one other hiker all day, John and his sidekick (his dog). We walked beside Benedict and Goose ponds as the miles clicked by, then we found our stop for the night in Lee, Massachusetts, on US 20.

Lee, Massachusetts

A gentleman named Scott gave us a ride to town, where we inquired about a room at two motels. Both ended up being owned by the same corporation. We took the most affordable rate and an upstairs corner room. Supper was at Rose's Restaurant, where I shoved down a chef salad with a pitcher of water.

We returned to Rose's the next morning. I had a favorite daybreak meal of blueberry pancakes. We walked past a Dunkin Donuts, and Jerry Zim gave us a ride back to the trail. We backpacked for nineteen miles up and over Becket and Warner Mountains before coming to a railroad track near Dalton, Massachusetts.

Dalton, Massachusetts

There was very little company on the white-blazed trail. We only saw hikers from Connecticut and Virginia, and there was John and Maria from Massachusetts. When we came into Dalton, the trail was a little tricky. We took a room at the Shamrock Motel. It was not very impressive, but the most accessible.

We went to the other side of town for pizza and a salad and did our laundry next door. Back at the motel room we watched the presidential debates between George W. Bush and John Kerry. It had been a beautiful day walking in the thick of God's creation, and the foliage was all the more brilliant.

After finding the trail the next day (it took a little navigation), we cut behind town and pointed our poles north. It was a Saturday. The quiet miles were behind us. We had a spectacular seventeen-mile trek leading up to Mount Greylock, with over ninety hikers and seven dogs crowding the trail.

Mount Greylock, Massachusetts

We had reservations at the Bascom Lodge (Biker's Garage) for ten dollars a night. When we went after the key, the manager graciously bumped us up to the lodge for the same rate. He said it was too cold down there in the garage. We just shook our heads in awe. It was 4 P.M., and we had time to clean up before a family-style meal was served.

We took a table in the corner booth for the evening and daybreak meals. Debbie and Katherine, a couple of ladies from Massachusetts who were day hiking, joined us. We all told each other about our families. Eric and I related our faith.

The meals were as great as the view from Mount Greylock. There were all kinds of hot teas and beverages. Family-style dishes were brought to the table with several courses to feast upon. We really were taking in the best of both worlds: the delights of the backcountry and joys around community tables.

Prune Picker and Arkansas Traveler outside the Bascom Lodge on Mount Greylock, Massachusetts.

Our plan was to hike through Sunday morning and find a church later in the day for a worship service. We encountered twenty-four hikers and even a few trail runners. (A trail runner packs light and runs the trail as a form of exercise. Few run the entire length.) We came into the next town by 12:30 P.M. under a steady rain.

North Adams, Massachusetts

A nice lady named Dorothy gave us a ride to the Holiday Inn, where we mapped out the day and secured affordable accommodations north of town. We ate a sandwich at a Subway, and then followed up on a contact Eric had at the Salvation Army, where we had dinner and a brief afternoon service.

The Captain of the Salvation Army church gave us a ride to the evening worship of First Baptist Church of North Adams. The pastopastor lived up in Vermont with his wife and large family. The people were friendly. It was all part of the adventure—a couple of strangers walking into unknown regions and seeking the necessities of life.

A couple from the church that night gave us a lift up the mountain to the cabin we had reserved. The cabin was rough. Prune Picker insisted on sleeping on the floor while I took the bed. The whole house was leaning off its foundation.

We woke up a little late the following day. It was 6:45 A.M. We were at breakfast at the nearby restaurant by 7:05. It was Monday morning, the eighth and the last day.

After a tasty treat of breakfast foods, we ventured to ask the only other patron there for a ride. Carol graciously agreed to take us back to the trail. She was going to hike up Mount Greylock for the day. She was a fourth-grade teacher in a community not far away. It was amazing that we found another hiker and that she was the only other person in the dining room at the time.

Bennington, Vermont

It was a soggy day beneath our feet but dry over our shoulders. We crossed into Vermont, climbed Harmon Hill, and came off the trail at Bennington, where we met Ken Stone (*Gray Panter*). We had traveled eighteen miles. Only four other hikers were on that link of the trail: a father and son, Matt from Washington D.C., and *Healed* from Maine.

Ken took us to Brattleboro for a dinner at the Mesquite Grill. He had been born and raised in the town. I was foot sore and stiff. Both *Prune Picker* and I were beat-up on the outside but refreshed on the inside.

Gray Panter took us all the way back to a motel in Hartford, Connecticut. That night it was good to be in town, clean, and able to look back on 122 miles. The woodland colors had been great. We took joy in added memories as good friends.

My oldest son, who had started the Appalachian Trail with me when he was eleven, was at that time serving in the U.S. Army. Here's a note *Prune Picker* wrote to him when he was about to be deployed to Iraq:

> *A couple of months ago your Mom and Dad*
> *sent me a camouflage bandana with Psalm 91*
> *printed on it. They asked us to keep it to*
> *remember to pray for you. It hangs at the end*
> *of our hallway as a regular reminder to lift*
> *you up to the Lord.*
>
> *Thanks for being over there and taking the*
> *war to the enemy. I pray that in your noble*
> *service you will find peace and purpose in*
> *Christ our Savior.*

*I have done three A.T. (Appalachian Trail)
hikes with your Dad...I know he could leave
me in the dust, but I keep putting one foot in
front of the other, and he keeps inviting me
back. Last fall we did 120 miles. We both
thank the Lord for reuniting our friendship,
which started in seminary in 1980.*

In His Spirit, Prune Picker

Prune Picker had the stuff. We were two of a kind that liked
adventure, loved mixing it up with people, and had hearts committed
to honoring the Lord.

There's nothing like a few mountain miles to test and build real
friendship. We always found, after adding a few more miles and a few
more blisters, that our bond had been tested and found to be even stronger,
and our faith all-the-more affirmed.

THE BLACK MUD OF VERMONT

The farther north you go on the Appalachian Trail, the more things change for a southern boy. One factor was finding the optimum hiking weather. The Green Mountain Hiking Club strongly recommended no hiking in May due to the mud on the trail and trail erosion.

Waiting until June meant rising temperatures and the ever-present New England pests (mosquitoes and black flies). I emailed my Vermont contact: *Gray Panter*. He did nothing but encourage me to come on as I planned. He agreed to provide the ride from Killington back to Bennington when I finished the weeklong hike.

I had never been to Rhode Island. Since I was within striking distance, I decided to fly into Providence, rent a car, and then drive to Bennington. In that way I could experience much of New England by interstates, country roads, and mountain trails.

On Sunday afternoon, I flew from Nashville to Atlanta to Providence. Travel always amazed me: on that single day I went from Tennessee to Georgia to Rhode Island, then to Connecticut, Massachusetts, and Vermont. When I arrived in Providence, I loaded my gear into a canary-yellow Chevy

Cobalt for the three-hour drive. The Vermont back roads were quiet between one and two in the morning.

I had a late breakfast at Jensen's Restaurant (Canadian bacon, eggs, wheat toast, and home fries). Before parking the yellow rental car back at the motel for the week, I went to a hardware store for stove fuel. The proprietor gave it to me. He said a lady bought a gallon the year before, only used a little, and told him to give it to someone else as needed. That is exactly what I had planned to do, since I could only use a small canister of fuel.

Kirk, the Asian Indian motel owner, gave me a ride mid-morning to the trail crossing. He told me a hiker had come in months before and left twelve hundred dollars' worth of gear to offset a motel bill he had. The hiker said he would never need the gear again.

Back on the trail, not expecting much company, I met two section-hikers: Dave and his dog, Beav (Beaver), and Jeff and his dog, Shelia. Jeff Brooks was an inner-city minister in Hartford, Connecticut. He was out backpacking for fifteen days. Jeff went to college in Colorado before making his home in the Hartford suburbs.

One thing he said stuck with me: "Trekking poles are like having two extra legs." He was right, especially when you're up to your ankles in black Vermont mud.

On that first day the terrain was fairly easy. It wasn't too hard of a climb up Glastenbury Mountain. A light rain and mist came down at the end of the day. It was a sign of what was to come that week.

The thirteen-mile day took me into the Kid Gore Shelters. It was not only wet, but also brisk. I spotted a porcupine at the shelter that night. The critter was black with gold quills. It was good to be out in the wilds again.

When the dawn came at 5:30 A.M., I was awake, but I stayed in the warm sleeping bag until 8 A.M. The night was restful, but rain, sleet and wind kept me hunkered down.

The Wet Green Mountains

I was on the trail by 9:15 A.M. It was cold and wet. The skies were heavy with sleet and snow as I crossed over the Green Mountains, where the Appalachian Trail and the Long Trail join and run upstate for about a hundred miles.

The trail was soggy, and it was difficult going rock to root in an attempt to stay dry. My boots and socks still got soaked. There were no hikers until Jeff came in the shelter around 6:20 P.M.

The Stratton Pond Shelter was fifteen miles north of the Kid Gore Shelters. All my gear was wet, except for one pair of socks and a few spare clothes. It had been a hard day in the sleet and mud, but I was aware of grace in every step across Stratton Mountain.

Psalms 143:8 was a Bible reference I noted that day: "Cause me to hear thy loving kindness in the morning; for in thee do I trust: cause me to know the way wherein I should walk; for I lift up my soul unto thee."

Wednesday morning came quickly, and I had twenty miles ahead of me. The trail would cross the Winhall River a couple of miles past the Stratton Pond. It would go over Spruce Peak and finally Peru Peak, where the shelter was located.

Along the way, it was busy for a weekday. I introduced myself to Lloyd, met groups of ten and eleven hikers, and then there was a lady professor and minister that went by the trail name *P.W.* (Pray and Work) and her lady partner, *Esau.*

On that day, I also saw a rabbit, smaller in size and with more fur than its southern cousins. He was a cute little varmint.

Time Warp

Peru Peak Shelter was very basic, like most Vermont shelters. Once again, I hung my gear out to dry, though it had not rained all day. The woods were wet, and the leaves were full of moisture from the previous drenching. I cooked a Lipton chicken noodle and broccoli dinner with a few crackers crumbled on top. It was delicious.

Once I cleaned up after cooking, it wasn't long before I was tucked in that warm sleeping bag. Time was warped. I began to think the sun rose at 2 A.M. and set by 6 P.M. On that day, I thought I scrambled out of the bedroll at 4 A.M. and that I had crashed the night before by 7 P.M. It was my wristwatch. It was behind by three hours.

The shelter was in front of a brook with a tent area next door. I was there solo. Low hanging limbs brushed up against the roofline at the Peru Peak Shelter that sounded like mice all night. The rain also gave the effect of scampering mice. There were a few in the shelter, but when I turned on my headlamp they were gone.

On the fourth day, I had some climbs on top of the Green Mountains. Just past Griffith Lake was Bakers Peak. Later, I eased past Little Rock Pond, crossed Vermont 140, and unloaded at Minerva Hinchey Shelter, another twenty-mile day.

The Professor and the Preacher

A section-hiker and I walked the last couple of miles into the shelter. The rains kept coming. I took the south end of the shelter to string up my wet clothes and poncho, while Bob McCaw, a PhD student in mathematics (a former lawyer), made himself at home on the north end.

The skies that day were gray, but it was the best day on the trail that week, because the rain waited until the tail end of the day.

I had an intriguing conversation with Bob. He was on his way to being a professor. As a preacher, I gently challenged him in the faith, and he gave it a modest hearing. We were worlds apart, yet we spent a solitary night in the Vermont Mountains under a shelter that kept us dry from the night's rainstorm.

Awake by 4:40 A.M., I rolled out of the sleeping bag while the songbirds stirred. I made a meal of bananas and cream oatmeal with crackers crumbled on top. I wrote an entry in the trail journal logbook (these are journals for hikers to write a few lines, date, and sign their names) while

Bob slept on. After I cleaned up the pan and packed up the backpack, I hit the trail by 6 A.M.

This was the last day. I was ready for a town meal and a shower. It had been a muddy and soggy weeklong hike, yet I was thankful for the grace that got me there. Here are a few lines that described the week walking through the heart of Vermont:

Black Mud in Vermont

All around me, spring is breaking out in the tree line
though the skies are black and gray as dark winter.
Beneath my boots is the black mud of Vermont.
It feels like a Texas oil slick crawling up my pant legs.

My waterlogged feet launch from rock to root,
seeking a way through the black lagoons of Vermont.
There's a log and here's a rock, and then it's a misstep,
so that where I had been dry before is real wet now.

It is a relief to find reprieve from the swampy trail,
yet finding solid ground is rare and so infrequent.
As the rains descend upon these Green Mountains
parts of the trail are impassable, so I cut into the woods.

There are very few footprints, but the ones I do see
are along the edge of the trail, big black irregular steps.
It goes on for miles and miles where the rains pound
the earth in a relentless downpour and deluge.

Somewhere behind dark clouds is a sun that shines;
beneath the mire are seeds that germinate new life.
The bog will soon give way to budding beauties
filling the landscape as life in the forest is reborn.

Killington, Vermont

It was another twenty-mile day climbing Beacon Hill and Killington Peak before I descended into the parking lot beside US 4, near Killington. The sun finally came out. I only encountered one section-hiker named Caleb. Near Cooper Lodge vandals had damaged the shelter and trail signs. The lodge was located in close proximity to a ski resort.

It was a pleasure to see the smile on Ken's face (*Gray Panter*) as he stood next to his purple Road Cruiser. For five days, I had slipped and slid over ninety miles in the black mud of Vermont. In order to make it out on time, I had to push hard all day.

My feet hit the gravel parking lot at 4 P.M. where I greeted Ken. We ate dinner at Jensen's in Bennington. Ken had a chicken breast sandwich and Coke, and I ordered a chicken salad and hot chai tea.

Back at the motel, I prepared for the next day. It would be a great way to top off the trip by driving the canary-yellow car back to Providence in the daylight. Spring was just now coming to the mountains. The Vermonters I spoke to told me the week had been unseasonably cold for late May.

As I loaded the trunk with my damp backpack in the morning, the sun was breaking out for good. Sunshine flooded the valleys as I drove past the Vermont farmlands and towns full of crafts and gift shops, nestled below the mountains I had hiked. I smiled at another week of memories and with the knowledge that Mount Katahdin was just a little closer.

Driving back to Rhode Island, I looked out of the windows at a neat and tidy world. The wilderness had been a real contrast to the buds and blooms of spring in New England town life. The muddy trails were messy and far from neat and tidy.

How does a backpacker deal with black mud and giant puddles? He presses on to the next mile marker.

Life is seldom neat and tidy. In fact, it can be black and muddy. There are times we stop and take in the beauty of the day, and then there are other times we press on through the black bogs until our feet reach green pastures and still waters. I was stretching for the green grass on top of that grand mountain in Maine where the trail touches the northern skies.

For, behold, the Lord cometh forth out of his place, and will come down, and tread upon the high places upon the earth. And the mountains shall be melted under him, and the valleys shall be cleft, like wax before the fire, and like the waters that are poured down a steep place. (Micah 1:3-4)

MAGIC ON MOOSE MOUNTAIN

It was time to finish Vermont and take on the White Mountains of New Hampshire. Ken Stone extended an invitation for a day of sailing before I went back on the trail. This friend from the trail was in his early sixties and was very active.

Besides being a snowboard instructor, he was also a sailor on Lake Champlain when the weather would permit. He enjoyed life to the fullest. He was an avid outdoor enthusiast. His wife, Nancy, was an accomplished artist and teacher.

Burlington, Vermont

I flew into Burlington to Ken's domain. The Stone's hospitality was more-than-gracious. Only another long-distance hiker could understand how indispensable such help can be. The first thing we did after leaving the airport was go to the lake.

It had the makings of a real adventure for a landlubber when we took the dinghy from the dock to the sailboat, anchored about 150 feet away. We prepared the craft for a short run and placed a few supplies and our backpacks in the cabin below.

119

Ken cast off the lines and started the motor. We eased out of the marina. On our right was Burlington scattered along a hillside, and on our left were the Adirondacks of New York. Just ahead lay a solitary island with a story to tell that reached back to the Revolutionary War.

On that island today, Vermonters still find cannonballs from colonial times. The rebels had planted a mast in the middle of that little piece of land. The Brits thought it was a ship and bombarded it all night during one of the battles in the region. When dawn broke, they realized they had been had by those ingenious and independent Americans.

The lake lies on the western edge of the state. That autumn evening everything was quiet and placid. We ate a snack of chips, salsa, and some crunchy carrots that Ken and Nancy had packed. Ken taught me a few basics about sailing and put me behind the large silver steering wheel.

We turned back to the harbor when the sun dropped behind the dark horizon. It was surreal. When we reached the mooring, Nancy looked back and caught her breath as she pointed to a bright orange moon. It was the perfect ending to a perfect sail.

We made our way across the frigid water to the dock. The three of us went to a deli, and ate next to a boardwalk and marina in town. I had a crab sandwich and blueberry-filled cookie. When we drove up to their house in Williston, we unloaded my heavy backpack and were greeted by Cedar, the Stone's golden retriever.

Stowe, Vermont

Before I went upstairs to my quarters, Ken and I made plans for the day to come. He was going to give me a tour of western Vermont. It was just as I had imagined and better. If I had another lifetime, Vermont would be a choice place to spend it. The glories of America are unending. God did some of his best work there in Vermont.

When that next day was done, I reflected on a day of pure pleasure:

- *Had a breakfast of blueberry pancakes and maple syrup.*
- *Enjoyed a hike in the woods behind the Stone's home.*
- *Visited Smuggler's Notch Snow Resort, where Ken worked.*

- *Experienced Stowe, Vermont, home of the Von Trapp family from The Sound of Music fame.*
- *Toured a cider shop and factory, and had a cider donut.*
- *Saw the original Ben and Jerry's Ice Cream Factory in Burlington.*
- *Shared the fascination of Nancy's art and art workbooks.*
- *Read Ken's Appalachian Trail journals and looked thru his photo highlights of the trail.*
- *Had a wonderful supper of Mexican lasagna with salad back at the Stone's home.*
- *Looked thru Alaska and Israel trip journals and artwork from the Stone's travels.*
- *Topped off a day to remember with vanilla ice cream and homemade raspberry bars.*
- *Talked of culture in Russia and other worldwide and cross-country travels.*

All of these pleasures would stand in stark contrast just twenty-four hours later. It was time to get down to the business of backpacking. When morning came, Ken and Nancy sent me off with oatmeal, blueberry muffins, a clementine, milk, orange juice, and toast with raspberry jam.

Killington, Vermont

We drove to Killington to US 4. I set my heart on the ten days ahead. My hope was to reach Mount Washington. It had a notorious reputation up and down the trail. In 1934 winds reached 231 mph, the highest wind velocity on record for the continent. Ken and I set our rendezvous spot for the top of Mount Washington—one I wouldn't make.

That day on the Green Mountain trail was beautiful to say the least. Twelve hikers were going south, and there were six in the shelter that night. I had missed the shelter signs for my intended destination and ended up hiking twice as far as I planned. Making my way in the dark under the first stars, I finished a twenty-mile day and made camp at the Wintturi Shelter.

There was a vacancy, but barely. As I squeezed in, I was introduced to Romnique and Ariel, a Jewish couple from Israel. Ed, from Wisconsin and Marshall, from New Jersey were old college friends out for an annual backcountry trip. They were also Jewish.

They were friendly and kind enough to insist I share their water rather than find my way to the water hole in the dark.

The last two hikers were Andrea and Mary. They were already in their sacks bedding down for sleep. I quickly fixed a Lipton noodle dinner and called it a day.

When morning broke, I was up early to prepare breakfast. I was sitting on an unstable wooden perch when Marshall sat down on the opposite end and sent everything into the black earth. He was very apologetic, but it was a disaster waiting to happen. The mishap was not his fault.

Taking a little more time to clean up and fill the water bottles, I said farewell and returned to the mountain trail.

Climbing Thistle Hill and Happy Hill, I passed nine hikers, including *Bemis* (the name of a mountain in Maine), and *Eft* (a type of salamander). Grouse was abundant. There were a few deer and playful chipmunks. They have the looks of a small squirrel and the spirit of a river otter. Life is all fun and chatter for a chipmunk.

As far as the *Arkansas Traveler*, it was another twenty-mile day, a duplicate of day one, hiking under the stars again. When I came to the Happy Hill Shelter, I met a couple, *Pumba* from Virginia and *Jungle Girl* from New Zealand. We exchanged basic biographical information and then they cuddled up and went to sleep.

Hanover, New Hampshire

The sun rose Friday morning on that late September day with the promise of Hanover and Dartmouth College just a few miles north. It was just six miles into town and that was all I did that day. When I reached the New Hampshire hamlet with the college green full of activity, I had run out of steam.

The day was a bust as far as hiking went, but I managed to find my way around after a little wandering. A professor of music (Jewish by faith) from the college gave me a ride to check out a couple of motels in the next town since the Hanover Inn was priced at over two hundred dollars a night.

After an unsuccessful jaunt, he dropped me off at EBA (Everything but Anchovies). I ordered a chef salad and water in the tightly packed cafe. I could not choke it down. It was good, but my stomach was not. The shelter the night before was short on water, so when I came to town, I waterlogged myself.

Finding a place for the night was going to be more of a challenge than climbing Mount Washington. I went to the Chamber of Commerce, hoping to get a lead.

There I reserved a room across the Connecticut River in White River Junction, Vermont, at the Hotel Coolidge. I waited an hour or so across the street from the college green for a free public transit to take me there.

White River Junction, Vermont

I was fortunate I didn't get into town late on that Friday. It would have been nearly impossible to find lodging. The hotel was built in the 1920's and named after Calvin Coolidge (whose home state was Vermont). The staff allowed hikers to stay for an affordable rate (thirty-two dollars a night) on the second floor. There were no elevators, just an old wooden stairway. It was like stepping nine decades back in time.

I took a shower and did my laundry. Walking a block downtown, I had supper at a pizza shop, still feeling a little queasy. The plan for the following day was to take a taxi six miles back to Hanover, have breakfast at Lou's Restaurant, and do a sixteen-mile day.

When Saturday came, I was back up and running at full throttle. After a hearty breakfast, I walked out of town, around a large athletic field, and accessed the trail behind some late morning snoozers who had their backpacking gear spread out everywhere near the edge of the woods.

It was a day of hiking in the sunshine. There were thirty hikers, nice views, long climbs, and some trail magic. On Moose Mountain, I shared lunch with five day-hikers, and a father and daughter from Delaware who called themselves *Pack Rat Two* and *Berks*. The day-hikers passed along some roasted almonds and a fresh flask of water (with ice cubes no less).

On the backside of the mountain, after taking a photo of another group of hikers at an overlook, I was closing in on Trapper John Shelter, where I planned to set up camp for the night.

I knew the shelter might be packed with weekend warriors that could prove a little rowdy. I prayed for an invitation off the trail with the hope of going to church the next day. That is exactly what happened in less than half-an-hour.

Lyme, New Hampshire

An older New Hampshire couple was out day-hiking. The lady was moving cautiously as her husband assisted her up the mountain. I was walking down the switchbacks less than a mile from the shelter where I intended to stop over for the night. After introducing myself, I asked a few questions before inquiring if they were believers. The lady's response surprised me. She said, "Praise the Lord."

That is not a typical New Englander reply. When they heard that I was a pastor, they promptly asked me to come home with them and join them for church in the morning. That was trail magic and divine providence wrapped in one. They were not sure why they decided to take that particular trail. It was a strain on her. Right away she said she knew why they were there—to meet me.

We agreed to a meeting place, and I hiked another three miles in wonder and awe. Roger and Chris Berger lived in a log home in Lyme, New Hampshire. They took me upstairs and invited me to make myself at home as they prepared dinner.

Around the table that night we had salad, pasta, broccoli, sweet corn, bread, and 2 percent milk. Dessert was vanilla ice cream and raspberries. (Food always tasted so good after hiking for eight-to-ten hours). It was an incredible joy taking in the Berger's Christian hospitality. What wonders God tucks into every day.

Thetford, Vermont

It was Sunday morning, and I woke up in a warm bed. Breakfast was not oatmeal on the trail, but bacon, waffles cooked with corn, eggs, and juice.

We went to church, where Roger taught a good Sunday School lesson. He also served as a deacon at the Thetford Baptist Church in Thetford, Vermont. It was a warm and young church in the kind of setting postcards capture in that part of the country.

The Berger's provided a quick lunch, and Chris fixed me up for the trail with snacks. They walked with me up the trail a few hundred yards along with a Chinese couple from their church: Han and Udy.

Sunday afternoon was a test of willpower. After a late start (2 P.M.), I had Smarts Mountain and a nine-mile hike ahead of me before I could call it a day. I counted nine other hikers that afternoon including Carey, a lady I had lunch with along with other hikers the day before on Moose Mountain.

Hexacuba Shelter was off the trail a little way. *Two-Step*, a Japanese-American college-aged lady from Cincinnati, Ohio, was in the shelter smoking a cigarette when I came in just before dark. Rains were coming in overnight.

I chatted with *Two-Step* for an hour or so and we both did some reading before we turned in for some shuteye. She asked me to look out for a few friends up the trail that she had hiked with in the weeks past and hoped to link up with again soon.

It was the only night I spent on the trail with a member of the other gender. Fortunately for both of us it was a spacious shelter. She had taken one side of one wall and when I came in, I took the other side of the shelter on the other wall to give her space. She told me there was a tent camper nearby, whom I never saw. I did what I could to put her at ease.

Monday was wet. I hiked Mount Cube and Mount Mist before hitting the road, NH 25 in Glencliff, and on to the Hikers Welcome Hostel. I saw only ten elderly day-hikers on that fifteen-mile stretch. When I came in, I met *Fat Chap* and *Pack Rat* who hosted the living quarters.

Glencliff, New Hampshire

Upstairs, I heard the trail saga of *Painfully Slow* from Jacksonville, Florida. She was a lady in her early fifties who was hiking north to south. Coming from Mount Katahdin, she tore her ACL (anterior cruces ligament) one of the first days out on the trail. She was hurting but pushing on.

Fat Chap took *Painfully Slow* and me into town to a little store and deli for supplies and a supreme pizza. On the way, we spotted a bear cub running beside the road for all he was worth. We returned and shared the pizza with *Huff and Puff* from New Jersey and *Planner* from Virginia, who were both middle-aged law enforcement officers who were doing a long-section hike.

It was a nice way to end a damp day, comparing notes with other hikers who were paying the price to take on a piece of the Appalachian Trail. The day had been wet but still nice, with rolling mists cast over mountain silhouettes.

That night I did my wet and dirty laundry, dried out the pack and gear, and added a few supplies to the food bag. *Painfully Slow* had just received a mail drop loaded with food and drink mixes—much more than she could carry in her backpack. So, she loaded me up with a few foodstuffs.

On Tuesday morning, I quickly packed and grabbed a leftover piece of pizza. *Huff and Puff* gave me a ride less than a mile to the place where the trail crossed the road. The day was tough. Backpacking over Mount Moosilauke at just under five thousand feet and then Mount Wolf, just shy of thirty-five hundred feet, made for a full day.

When dusk came, I was still hiking and I was a little weary, ready for some rest. Only five hikers were on the trail, but the Eliza Brook Shelter was maxed out with youth from a local school along with their two instructors. There was no room. Trail etiquette said thru-hikers get the first dibs on a shelter, then section-hikers.

These youth and their teachers were in violation and most likely did not know it. It was a good thing it was just me. I knew thru-hikers who would have had some choice words if they had run up against such inconsideration. It was a very rough shelter, but still it was the only one for another six miles. Most school groups would tent camp.

The young lady teacher offered the kitchen tarp as a makeshift tent and cover from the rain. I slept there on the ground pitched a few dozen feet away from their wilderness camp. I checked my attitude and made the best of it after a seventeen-mile day. It was cold, but thankfully I slept well and took off after the break of day.

The first signpost gave mileage information for the Appalachian Trail. The second read: "This trail is extremely tough. If you lack experience please use another trail. Take special care at the cascades to avoid tragic results."

Traveling just twelve miles, I had a trial and error experience in finding my way. I opted out of my plan to stay at one of the famous New Hampshire huts when I heard the price, though I did have lunch at the Lonesome Lake Hut.

Expecting a work-to-stay arrangement, I found out it was not available to section-hikers. The workers at the hut did offer all-you-can-eat soup for two dollars. Apple-spice muffins and lemonade added another dollar.

After hiking South and North Kinsman Mountains, I searched for another place to lodge. There was no lodging nearby when I crossed US 3, so I went up the next mountain to Liberty Springs tent sites, hoping for a shelter of some kind on that cold and wet night. I counted eighteen hikers that day.

Fortunately, a kind-hearted Canadian named Bob Holland (Ontario) offered me a spot under his tarp on a tent platform. His partner snored, so he was at another platform in order to get some quiet rest.

We shared about our family life, and he picked up right away that I was a minister from my line of questioning. We slept soundly. It was great to be dry as well as warm.

The Franconia Ridge

In 124 days on the trail, there wasn't a day quite like the next one. No hike compared in any of the previous twelve years. I can never forget it. First, it was rainy and windy. I crossed many blow downs (uprooted trees from high winds) with moss and roots from spruce trees entwined and uprooted all across the ridgelines.

Second, the trail was desolate with only four hikers. The walk was on what was called the Franconia Ridge, and the winds were so ferocious that day that they reached 60 mph as I climbed Little Haystack, Mount Lincoln, Mount Lafayette, and finally Mount Garfield. I had come to the Presidential Mountains on a very uninviting day. They lived up to their reputation.

The winds were so strong they blew me sideways, sent me to my knees over and over, and blew my pack cover off twice. I could only grit and bear it (as opposed to "grin and bear it"). It was punishing. Sheer will and God's grace alone got me across the granite trail fully exposed to the windstorm. Then it rained.

Galehead Hut

When I stumbled into Galehead Hut at 2:30 P.M., I was soaked. Everything in the pack was wet. It was less than eleven miles, but I was ready to call it quits for the day. Jim Kerry was there, a hut-to-hut hiker on a break from his restaurant business. He had retired as a teacher after thirty-five years in Cape Cod, Massachusetts.

The Appalachian Mountain Club workers (they ran the hut system in New Hampshire) were very gracious with ample soup that warmed my insides. Then they heaped on a mountain of kindness by including me for supper and breakfast around the table (it was just Jim and me there).

I spent the afternoon getting my gear dried out for the final day on the trail. God's grace had been evident everywhere that stormy day, especially when the heavy cloud cover broke, so I could see the world below from the windy heights of Mount Lafayette.

Friday morning came all too quickly, and I had to talk myself out of the warm bunk. It was frigid. I took a rinse in the sink and packed up. Around the table I enjoyed oatmeal with toppings of granola, raisins, and brown sugar.

I was out into the winter wonderland by 8 A.M. It was all uphill to South Twin Mountain and a heavy frost covered the top of all the ridges and signposts that marked the trail.

After Mount Guyot, I had all-you-can-eat creamy soup at Zealand Falls Hut around 12:30 P.M. On the way down to Ethan Pond just past the hut, I took a hard fall on some very slick rocks (what gratitude I had that nothing was broken). I counted twenty-two hikers. The section from Zealand Falls to Crawford Notch was one of the most memorable ones on the Appalachian Trail, and it was a fairly even grade to US 302.

There was thrill and adventure in walking the White Mountains solo in the early mornings when the frost covered the signposts and cairns (stacks of rock to mark the trail). What a time of real contemplation and drinking in the experiences of the wilderness.

Crawford Notch, New Hampshire

The colors of fall were in full array, and the scenery reminded me of the trails out west. I had to hoof it and make double time in order to meet Ken for our rendezvous at 4 P.M. He was waiting for me. We drove to the Crawford Notch Appalachian Mountain Club Lodge and Store. It was a fabulous facility.

We could see Mount Washington and a panoramic view of the Presidential Mountains by traveling farther west on US 302. I had fallen shy of the noble mountain by only twelve miles.

As we drove back toward Vermont, we saw a dog cloud star formation (which are ice crystals reflecting off the sun in the sky). It appeared as if it were an apparition in the distant sky, white and ghost-like against the light blue heavens. This is something I had never heard about or seen before.

Montpelier, Vermont

Ken and I ate in Montpelier at La Beau Cafe, a culinary training restaurant. I had a veggie quiche pie with a couple of rolls and a chai latte. Before our departure from the quaint capital of Vermont (population eight thousand), we scoped out the government buildings. We came into Williston, the Stone's home place near Burlington at 7:30 P.M., and I went straight to the shower.

When I came downstairs, Nancy served a homemade apple pie and ice cream. Later, I had a second piece with cheese and a cup of apple cider. Hospitality was never better anywhere. We tuned into part of the Red Sox and Yankee game in the World Series match-up. I was in Red Sox country.

My sixteen-year-old daughter sent me a note for those ten days in the Green and White Mountains:

> *Dad: I hope you will have a wonderful hiking*
> *trip. I would love to be climbing and killing*
> *myself with you, but I have to be here.*
> *Anyways, I hope one day I can go and see what*
> *the A.T. is all about. I pray you'll be a spark or*
> *should I say a blaze of fire when you return. I*
> *know you love to go and see with new eyes. I*
> *will be thinking and praying for you. Where*
> *are you now? Passing through the Kentucky*
> *air? Vermont? I love you and will miss you. Be*
> *safe and may our Father bless and protect you*
> *each day...Have an awesome time.*
> *Karis, Psalm 91.*

Such love and prayer were better than a Lipton noodle dinner, a nine-to-ten-hour night's rest, and standing on top of a mountain's majesty. It gives a man the extra ump he needs to overcome when he's footsore, soaked to the bone, or waking up to the chill of the wilderness.

The trail from Zealand Falls to Crawford Notch reminded me of hiking the Rockies out west. Here is a look to the north with hiking poles and the backpack leaning on a boulder along the smooth path leading to Crawford Notch.

Life on the trail was much like the elevations a backpacker experienced: The delights of the mountaintops through grueling climbs to the quiet vales—all of it was part of the story of grit and glory. Motivation became the issue.

What moved the long-distance hiker over long and lonely miles? In part, it was the thrill of each town stop, the untapped promise in every human encounter, and the gratification from standing on another mountaintop.

While my boots made tracks across the mountain trail for those ten days and 143 miles, I wrote down a few thoughts at camp while the last light of the sun faded on the distant peaks. These lines capture a few of the moments I would never forget.

Mountain Apple Orchard

Hard days and long miles
on the Vermont highlands
tax my body and mind.
Chocolate loses its appeal,
I turn to trees along the trail,
old, gnarly apple trees.

They are tart and riddled
with a multiple of dark spots,
yet there's enough flavor
to punch me another mile or two.
So, I load up my pockets
with three mountain apples.

Makes me smile as I think about
early American pioneer,
Ole Johnny Appleseed.
More than likely a farmer
planted these mini-orchards,
nothing wrong with wondering.

Curse the Wind

This wind is insidious, ferocious, and relentless.
It is nearly murderous as I take on the bare heights.
Clouds blow like monstrous vapors full of darkness.
The wind tosses me, scares me, just about picks me up.
I fight, shout, resist, push, and curse the wind:
I shout, "Dadgum you wind." Then comes round-two.

Eyebrows Blown Sideways

Windy mountaintops can sometimes be hard—scrambled.
My trekking poles are two more legs to keep balanced.
My body is blown nearly parallel with the stony trail.
My eyebrows go sideways with the gusts fit for air travel.

The wind whips and whines against body, mind, and soul.
It is just about all I can do to take one more step forward.
On the downside of the trail the trees are a wind shield.
The pack cover flies off, hiking today is an extreme sport.

That Last Mile

The hardest and longest mile is the last one.
It is the one that rolls on forever and ever.
You keep expecting that this is it, almost there.
But no, the stopping place still eludes
and calls the weary traveler on, further on.
The feet stumble, you suck in wind,
and the mind thinks about nothing but pack off,
boots untied, dry clothes, warmth,
a supper meal and sweet sleep undisturbed.
Before the promise of calling it a day,
first comes every step in that final endless mile.
It is grueling, cruel, demanding,
and without much mercy, still it goes on and on
to the infinity of sunset and into the night
when the headlamp comes out.
From white blaze to white blaze, you pray
not to miss the sign that marks the way
to the shelter, where a little company awaits
in a haven of rest just after the last mile.

Tired beyond Telling

Forewarned of the treachery of these
White Mountain miles,
I am still determined to go the distance.
My body is pushed again and again
beyond comfort and reason.
I hike late—beyond the sunset,
and I hike at times with gritted teeth
to make the next mile marker.
When I reach home for the night,
I am not only tired, but spent,
not only spent, but too tired to talk,
and that is tired beyond telling.

Gray Panter at a trailhead in Vermont. He was an incredible help in Vermont, New Hampshire, and Maine in working out the logistics for three section-hikes. He and his wife, Nancy, treated their guests like family. I will forever remember them for their kindness and hospitality.

Thy mercy, O Lord, is in the heavens; and thy faithfulness reacheth unto the clouds. Thy righteousness is like the great mountains; they judgments are a great deep: O Lord, thou preservest man and beast. (Psalm 36:5-6)

THE MAHOOSUC CHALLENGE

Every adventure has its rough spots. A backpacker can expect there to be adverse conditions and less than perfect days when things go wrong. I had been warned that May was not an optimum month to finish the White Mountains and trek into southern Maine. I should have listened.

When I flew into Burlington, Vermont, to meet *Gray Panter*, I had mapped out 157 miles from Crawford Notch, New Hampshire, to Stratton, Maine. I didn't make it to Stratton. Though spring was in full bloom in Tennessee, it was still wintertime in the White Mountains.

Gray Panter drove me across his state and into the Presidential Mountains for a ten-day-hike across the sixty-four miles remaining in New Hampshire and into Maine, the fourteenth and final state on the Appalachian Trail. Rains had been sweeping the northeast at record rates, and I had high hopes that sunny days were on their way.

Seven of the next nine days on the trail were wet. I encountered conditions that I had never faced before: massive snow drifts, icy rocks for miles, and fallen alpines strewn across most of the next ninety miles into the northern wilds. It would be nothing less than an endurance test. For the most part, I had it all to myself.

Before I hit the highlands, Ken and I had a Quiznos sandwich. The day was wet and cold. It took four-and-a-half hours to hike six miles. The trail was soggy, and it was the first day of many that I got soaked. Nobody else was out there.

One of the advantages of hiking during or after a rain is that it does provide a little stealth for quiet steps through the woods. Even so, I was a bit surprised when a jackrabbit came right at me down the trail chased by a pine marten (a rare sight). They quickly split ways when they spotted me—the rabbit lived another day, and the pine marten took to a tree.

I reached Mizpah Hut at about 6:10 P.M. and pulled off my wet gear. Dave Anderson, the caretaker was there.

He had plans to study for his Master's in History or English at the University of New Hampshire in the fall. We talked about his background and issues of personal faith. He was kind enough to let me dry out my gear by the two big iron stoves in the kitchen. The tea hit the spot and I partook of some bakery goods.

Mount Washington

The next day would be a real stretch. I would need truckloads of grace to get over Mount Washington and press on to Pinkham Notch by nightfall. I was on the trail by 7:15 A.M., climbing Pierce, Franklin, Washington, and Madison. The sun peaked out a little behind a gray overcast sky. The winter snow was in big frozen flows across the sides of the mountains.

About 6 P.M. the rain started coming down. I trudged on until 9 P.M., when I reached the notch in the dark. Fortunately, the college-aged workers at the Joe Dodge Lodge (which was running over with school children) called the dining hall for a late supper. There had not been a single hiker on the trail all day—only one crazy trekker climbing those frosty highlands.

It had been a twenty-mile day and fourteen hours of hiking. I determined not to do any more days like that. The lady in the dining room gave me generous portions of supper—so much I could not get it all down. I dried out my gear and took a little time to call my sweetheart. The realities of the trail were beginning to curtail any previous plans.

The morning came quickly, and it was wet. I enjoyed breakfast in the dining hall and got back on the trail. The six miles that day were long and laborious. I was off the trail by 2:30 P.M.

Annie, the caretaker at Carter's Notch, told me that a father and daughter had covered the same distance four days earlier and it took them twelve hours to do it. They were experienced backpackers, and the daughter had climbed a number of the higher elevations in the region.

The conditions were dismal with mud, ice, and rain. Trees were down everywhere. I did meet a couple of day-hikers in the morning on Wildcat Peak A—John and Lorraine from New York. They would be one of the few sets of hikers I would see on the entire trek.

It was nice to be dry and warm by the potbelly stove. The rains kept coming down outside the hut. Blue skies finally appeared around 4:30 P.M. I was still glad I was in for the night.

Annie fixed some organic food (kelp and soybean squares). I ate like I was famished and drank hot tea in ample portions. I left as much of a tip as I could for Annie's hospitality.

My host had her living quarters behind the kitchen and dining area, while the backpackers went out back to a couple of cabin bunkhouses. That night I had all kinds of space and absolute quiet as I slept in a dry bunk.

On Friday morning, I fixed oatmeal in the hut kitchen and a cup of hot tea before quietly exiting for the day's hike. It was all uphill to Carter's Dome, and then down came my old nemesis—the rain. I got soaked and prayed for deliverance. I fought ice, snowdrifts up to my waist at times, slick rocks, roots, and steep grades.

The snowdrifts were heavy and deep, especially going up the last few tenths of a mile onto a peak and going the first few tenths of a mile back down a mountain. I pulled off the trail early (1:00 P.M.) because the rain kept coming. I had hoped to walk another seven miles into Gorham, New Hampshire. Imp Shelter provided a reprieve from the torrential rainfall.

I thought I would have it to myself since hikers were so scarce. Surprises are never-ending when you take a walk in the wilderness. I had just pulled on dry clothes and found places to hang all the wet ones, as well as my poncho, when I heard voices. A gang of college men from Pennsylvania, New York, and Maine invaded the one dry spot in the forest.

It was great to have the company. These young men were dressed in sweatshirts and jeans. (Experienced backpackers stay away from heavy clothing because of factors like rain and humidity.) A couple of them had no dry clothes. They were shivering from the cold.

I made room, and they threw off soaked tennis shoes, socks, clothes, and crawled into wet sleeping bags. They were out for ten days and this was day one.

There was Pete (*Centaur*), John (*Trail Pacer*), Calvin (*Trailblazer*) and Jason (*White Moth*). We talked a little, and I found out that Jason was a believer. A couple of the guys asked if I would mind if they smoked some pot—they didn't call it pot. I told them it was their call. Instead they stepped out in the woods in-between the rain showers.

We had just finished supper when we heard more voices coming from the wet woodlands. A group of high school students and a couple of adults came into the shelter soggy and miserable. One young lady was on the brink of tears.

We made room on the bottom level so they could get out of the rain. We went topside. They hung their wet things on the front porch of the shelter.

They were all from a coastal town in Maine. A coach named Stacy served as their leader. He was assisted by a parent (Cynthia), the mother of Cameron, one of two young men in the group. The other young man was Matt, and the young lady was Jolene. She was so wet, beat, and nerve-racked she did not feel like eating the coach's tasty-looking noodle supper.

We were all fairly dry and drifted off to sleep as the rains pounded away on the roof of the little shelter packed with ten people now. One of the college guys from Maine carried a fifty-pound pack with everything in it. When I had come into the shelter that afternoon, there was a CamelBak water bottle and tent left there—he added those to his pack too.

Gorham, New Hampshire

I awoke with a faint hope for sunshine that Saturday morning. Though it was hard to accept hiking just seven-mile days—that was all I planned to do so I could get into Gorham and do laundry, re-supply, and call home. Up by 5 A.M., I was on the trail by 6:30 A.M. When I crossed US Highway 2, I managed after a mile or two to get a ride into town.

Luke, a student at Bates College in Maine, was the Good Samaritan. Once I was in town, I unbuckled my pack and set it and my hiking poles in a Subway restaurant booth, and ordered a chicken salad sandwich and raspberry drink. After asking around, I found Hiker's Paradise, where I did my laundry and took a nap.

They said I was the first north bounder they had seen that year. I understood why after experiencing the conditions of the trail. It was my first day without rain on the trail—though it did rain once I got into the hostel. After the nap, I cleaned up my gear, bought some snacks, and ate supper at a Chinese restaurant.

The eight miles into town had been a little rough, but it smoothed out as I got closer to the highway. I did have to ford two streams, one of which was a heart-stopper. My boots died that day too. They came apart on top at the toes. The rain had done the job. Those Cabela's specials had gone at least a thousand miles since Virginia.

It was Sunday. I had hunted for a church and finally found a retired Baptist minister who would give me a ride after breakfast into the next town: Berlin. The Hiker's Paradise had a good breakfast. I ordered from their menu, as I looked out on Highway 2, which cut through Gorham. I feasted on waffles and blueberries with a glass of milk.

The Community Bible Church was a friendly congregation. They had bought an old Catholic church and made some major renovations. It was "Missions Day" and there was an American missionary speaker that served in the Philippines. The retired pastor's son and his family took me home for a great meal of ribs, veggies, and an ice cream sandwich.

Jack and Alice were raising support to move to Florida where Jack would serve as a computer tech for New Tribe Missions. Jack gave me a ride to the trail, and Alice sent an apple for the afternoon. Such people made even hard times on the trail worthwhile.

Because my boots had died, I put on my amphibian shoes. Before I even hit the woods, it started raining. For the fifth day I got soaked.

I came into Gentian Camp Shelter by 8 P.M., after a twelve- mile hike. It had a fantastic view of a ravine full of rapids that overlooked a valley below. It was cold, and I was alone. As my clothes were drying out, I snuggled under a fleece lining I had brought in Harpers Ferry for the sleeping bag—so glad I made that purchase.

It was a teriyaki chicken noodle dinner night. I needed a good night's sleep and my belly full for what awaited me the next day. It would be my roughest day on the entire trail. It was time to cross into Maine and take on the Mahoosuc mile. It was a challenge in the best of conditions, but then you add fallen trees, icy boulders, and snow up to your armpits—it would be a test indeed.

The Mahoosuc Mile

There was one blessing that came with the sunrise: no rain. The mountaintops that day were cold and windy. The trail was not well-marked once I entered Maine. Though I had been spared blisters and injuries up to that point, the Mahoosuc mile required some of my blood. It has been called the toughest mile on the entire Appalachian Trail.

Full of giant boulders, the white-blazed trail romped across an obstacle course with four or five notches. The backpacker must send his poles through the notch in the boulder, and then take off his backpack and push it through the passageway. Only then can he himself squeeze through to the other side.

The trail went blind at one point, and I had to take quite a bit of time to double back and check every possible route before I found it. When the mile was finished, I had skinned my fingers and just about broken my leg on one fall. It was slick, icy, and treacherous. I was left with a nine-inch abrasion just below my left knee.

God gave me grace in the boulders, and I would need more grace as the day came to a close. I spotted a camp of four or five people and their dogs off the trail and kept moving. I was hoping to make Speck Pond Campsite—but it was not to be. The trail went blind again. There was not a white blaze for much of the trail going up the Mahoosuc Arm.

I climbed the 3,770-foot mountain as the weather began to turn cold and snowy. The trail played out, so I doubled back. It was getting late by that time. I decided to call it a day, still not sure if I was on the trail or not. It was too late to climb the mountain again before dark. It had been a day for praying. Now I looked to heaven for shelter.

God was there in the shadows giving a little light in the madness of that frosty night. I had spotted a rock with a little wiggle room underneath on one of my searches for trail markers. When I came upon it again, I pulled the pack off. The thirteen-mile day seemed much longer, and that number was not counting all the backtracking.

The place under the rock shelter was tight and sloped, but it would do the next nine hours. My clothes were damp and wet from the day before, so I changed into the dry ones from my pack. I took out the sleeping pad and bag, then found the stove and food supplies, and cooked supper. The poncho served as a screen on the open side toward the trail.

Out of those twenty-four hours came these lines from my trail journal:

Mahoosuc Murder Mile

It is notorious. It is bloody. It is a worthy challenge.
They call it the toughest mile on the Appalachian Trail.
The Mahoosuc Notch lives up to its rugged reputation.
Climbing boulders with a loaded pack is precarious.
And I'm doing it in haphazard winter conditions.
Downed alpines and a rough trail add to the mix, too.
I give blood more than once in the series of notches.
High adventure is a wonderful thing. My timing is not.
The notches are so tight at times that I have to get skinny.
I size up the huge boulder. Poles are thrust through first.
The backpack is squeezed forward through the way north.
Not so unlike life itself. We do not pick the circumstances.
Get down to the essentials and get skinny. Push through.
Most of all, we watch every step or we give more blood.
Life's a scramble. At times it's a long boulder climb.

A Night in the Forest

It's a thirteen-hour day, hiking icy mountain trails.
The frozen journey includes a mile-long boulder run.
Once I pass the formidable challenge, the trail goes blind.
I climb Mahoosuc Arm and double back, hunting the trail.
Daylight fades and the only shelter I can find is a rock.
On the side of the trail, I roll under a stone outcropping.
Taking off my wet clothes, I change into dry ones.
I locate the stove, fuel bottle, and the noodle supper next.
Finding the pad, sleeping bag, I stretch out at an angle.
Poncho and pack provide a screen from the trail.
My food bag lies nearby, squeezed under the rock shelter.
About 10 P.M., I drift off to sleep under a wool fleece.
It's a long hard night, but I'm back on the trail by sun up.
My night in the forest is not the stuff of romance or song.
Yet, I learn that God is my refuge in times of trouble.

It was a light sleep. I still woke up refreshed. It was cold. There had been a little snowfall, and the poncho was frozen. Once I mustered up the motivation to move, I changed back into the damp clothes (this may sound loco, but most backpackers seek to keep one set of dry clothes in reserve), ate a quick snack, and packed up. I prayed I would find the trail, make it to the road, and then find a ride to Andover.

As I made my way north, I discovered that I was on the trail in spite of the scant markers. If there was ever a place on the Appalachian Trail to be sure the blazes were clear, that was the place.

The first mile or so I came to Speck Pond. I actually saw a group of three fully outfitted men going south. I asked if I could buy a little trail food from them since I was running short. As a diabetic, I always wanted to be sure not to get caught without a food source. One of the men gave me some trail mix and beef jerky.

Two other backpackers came down the trail. All five men had been at Speck Pond campsite overnight. There were some pleasant spots as

I walked toward Grafton Notch. The conditions were still slick. When I came to the parking lot at the Notch, there was a group of rowdy high school youth with their elderly lady bus driver. They directed me to Andover, a well-known trail town in southwest Maine.

Andover, Maine

Across the mountain Andover was eighteen miles, but by road it was more like twenty-eight miles. I had already walked eleven miles to the parking lot and preferred not to walk too many miles on pavement.

A mile down the road I spotted a couple sitting at a roadside park. He had written, "She said 'Yes'" on the side of his economy car. I asked about a ride to Andover, Maine. They weren't going my way so I smiled and said, "Congratulations."

They thanked me, and I went on—looking half the vagabond and half the weary trekker. After hoofing it on the pavement for about a mile, a couple of day-hikers gave me a ride to Hwy 5, which led to Andover.

Then within minutes of putting out my thumb while walking on Highway 5, Richard Gallant picked me up and took me the rest of the way. He agreed to shuttle me the next morning back to Grafton Notch, so I could cover the ten miles to the place where the trail came near Andover. It was a quaint town, and I felt at home the next two days.

I was all alone upstairs in the Andover Guesthouse. A beautician downstairs came out of her shop and showed me around. It was nice to get unpacked and cleaned up.

I had lunch and supper across the road in a country store. That night I caught up in the journal, did some reading, and called family. Then I took in a movie downstairs.

The decision was made to cut my trip short by a day. *Gray Panter* would be picking me up early in two days. I could only get one more day's hike in without holding him up from a commitment he had made back in Vermont.

When morning came to Andover, Richard took me to Grafton Notch, and I hiked the ten miles back toward town. It was a pleasant day, cold on the heights and summer-like in the vales. It rained up on West and East Baldpate Mountains.

The rains were not heavy enough to require a poncho, though the winds were fierce on the higher elevations. I just pulled the hood from my light jacket over my head when I needed cover from the rain.

There were no other hikers. The flowers had begun to come out: purple, white, and yellow mountain varieties of trillium. I plucked a few samples to press in the trail Data Book for my wife. The wind was chilly, so I kept on the move.

Lunch was at Frye Notch Lean-to. I had a ham and cheese sandwich prepared at the deli in the country store in Andover.

Though I saw all the tracks and droppings of the evasive moose, I did not sight one on the trail for those eighty-nine miles in nine days on the trail. I did scare up a dove and a grouse or two. Toward the end of that last day, there was a spectacular waterfall.

It was Dunn Notch and Falls. Unfortunately, it was well traveled with signs and blazes everywhere. The overlook reminded me of an overrun campground.

I came to the gravel road thirty minutes early where I waited for Richard. It was eight miles back to Andover. The mosquitoes started buzzing, looking for a late lunch on my ears.

Richard drove up in his white pickup truck right on time so my blood loss was minimal. I tried to pay him a fair price while saving enough money to get back home with for the remaining three days. He refused to take more than twenty dollars for gas.

It had rained for three weeks in New Hampshire and Maine. It was good to be finished this time around. I had fallen short by some sixty-eight miles. There were 257 miles to go before Katahdin. Back at the hostel, I cleaned and packed up my gear, then went for supper. The evening was spent reading articles on the trail in the library downstairs.

Gray Panter would be in for a mid-morning pick-up the next day. It was a four-hour drive for him from western Vermont. I would have a couple of days with him, enjoy the Stone's hospitality and their great cooking, take in a Friday morning Bible study at his church, and then fly south on Saturday at the break of dawn.

There were challenges yet to come on the Appalachian Trail—I was sure of it. For a section-hiker who could have picked any time of the year to access the trail, I had not done so well. But just being in Maine was an accomplishment after the slow grind through the thirteen other states in over thirteen years of doing the trail. It was all very worthwhile. Every day and every stop were now a treasured memory.

Without a doubt, this trek had been the most daring. Walking all alone on the snowy mountain tops, feeling like an Antarctica explorer at times, pushing on past miles of snow and ice, reaching the last state on the long trail, then crossing the notorious Mahoosuc boulder field, all made for a National Geographic kind of adventure.

Perhaps mere grit could get you across such treacherous territory, but I was glad I had grace from above for every icy step, too.

Spring Snow Flows

*It's disconcerting. Steps venture across large snowfields
sloping down the White Mountains of New Hampshire.
How solid is this ground? What if it were to give way?
Can I arrest my fall if I step on an ice slick this high up?
All these questions orbit my mind, as I pick out the path
across the snowbound Presidential Range of New England.*

*We're already into spring by two full months, yet winter
still has the Whites locked down. No one at all is up here.
Faint tracks from previous travelers cut across the snow.
No wildlife stirs in this ice land, except a bird or two.
I'm alone with the Creator on top of a white world.
Somewhere a few elusive moose are romping about.*

*On the mountains, the hiker battles ice, rain, snow, mud,
while spring breaks through with flower and bud.
Here above the gray clouds, sunshine has not smiled on
this part of the world for days and weeks and months.
Looking north, I listen to the pounding heart of the wilds,
and I hear my own heartbeat, walking the frosty heights.*

Under Rain Clouds

Seven days out of nine have been soaked in rain.
The other two have produced snow and a winter mix.
Mud is ankle deep. The frozen stuff prevails.
Rocks are slick. Roots are like running boards downhill.
This is spectacular country, even with a canopy of clouds.
Records are being set in rainfall, and nobody is trekking.
Moisture silences my steps. Wildlife are unaware I'm here.
Color means everything: Gray and black are out.
Blue is definitely in. Blue skies are like an old friend.
They been away too long. The sunshine is like family.
She's been far and away. We're past due for golden rays.

THE KATAHDIN MAGNET

It was time to finish. A mountain in north central Maine was calling my name. There, above the wilds, Mount
Katahdin marked the end of the long journey. This was the last Appalachian Trail section hike. I started on the East B Hill road near Andover, eight miles from town.

Fourteen years had come and gone since my sons and I set out from Springer Mountain in Georgia. Along the white blazes that marked the trail, I had eleven hiking partners, and one more would be added on this final trek.

Maine was considered a challenging state, notorious for an array of bugs: black flies, mosquitoes, and deer flies. In what could easily be tagged "the bug state," I had allotted seventeen days to walk from Andover to Katahdin, a stretch of 257 miles. There were at least thirty-two mountains in this section.

It was late June, and summer had come to the state after only a few short weeks of spring-like weather. The snow and ice had melted, and the bugs and heat were hard realities by the time I arrived.

Back to Andover

On my return to Andover, I took a night's lodging at Pine Ellis, hosted by Paul and Illene Trainor. At the local post office, I mailed a small backpack and duffle bag to Monson for an end-of-the-trail pickup. Fortunately, the Trainors had some fuel for my WhisperLite backpacking stove.

Supper was shepherd's pie, a salad, and green tea at a country store in the tiny town. The next morning, I returned to the store for a stack of blueberry pancakes and cold milk before hitting the backcountry. It was time to leave life among the populous and camp out with the stars and shadows in the wilderness passes.

There is no place on earth like the mountains. Time in the highlands always put my heart at rest. That first day I hiked eleven hours, fell six times while getting my trail legs back, and as usual, I met a few characters along the way.

There was *Mr. Cow Pie* and his daughter, *Twisted Sister*, from Kentucky. His actual work was to entertain school children on his farm back home. Next there was *Orange Blaze* and *Trocar* (which I learned later was an embalming tool). They were quick step thru-hikers and hailed from New York and Pennsylvania.

Then, I met a gentleman that had been on the trail since 1967. His home was in Amsterdam, but he was originally from Scotland. *Traveler* was famous, unconventional, and tough as nails, hiking the Appalachian Trail up and down for an undisclosed number of times.

Other thru-hikers included *Stoker, Cave Man,* and *Salty Dog*, and their dog, Bo, all from Texas. There were three section-hikers at the shelter that night: *Wild Bird* from New York, *Slowly-but-Surely* from Florida, and *Gigi*. The last one was a great-grandmother from the Show Me State (Missouri). She had six children, twenty-three grandchildren, and six great-grandchildren with two more on the way.

On day one, there were beautiful vistas and a gentle rain fell. It had been a nineteen-mile day. Six of us rolled out our sleeping bags side-by-side and slept in the cramped shelter: three men and three ladies. The other two men were Orange Blaze and Trocar.

Wild Bird, one of the ladies, wasn't too happy when she stepped in dog poo. Who would be after a long day on the trail when you're ready to relax a bit? The stuff of humanity and divinity are all too evident out there along the mountain trails when you go from the mountain marvels to the realities of dog poo.

An hour after sunrise (6 A.M.), I was the first hiker out, but *Orange Blaze* and *Trocar* soon overtook me. They had the strides of men who had been out there for a while and were reaching for the end. These young men were my rabbits for several days, as I sought to stay within a half a day behind them. They ended up finishing a couple of days ahead of me. On that second day there were no big mountains, so I covered twenty miles before camp.

Around the shelter that night we had a father and son, who were climbing 110 mountain peaks in the northeast, *Orange Blaze* and *Trocar*, and Greg from Georgia, a section-hiker on the trail for twenty-one years. He hoped to finish the trail that time, just as I did.

During the hike that summer day, I had also met *Tau*, the first lady thru-hiker going north for the year. She was on her own turf in Maine, where she had built her house and a garage. I also spotted a red fox coming down the trail in the morning hours.

Day three was a four-mountain day. I fought a drop in blood sugar and at times had double vision. Saddleback Junior Mountain was notable. I traveled seventeen miles and met a group of teens and twenty-somethings: *Hot Pursuit* from Maine, *Prancer* and *Teapot* from Pennsylvania, a young lady, *Twix* from Massachusetts, and later on I met *Thorny* from Virginia. *Thorny* was a middle-aged gentleman and a thru-hiker going south.

That night at the shelter I bought snacks from *Orange Blaze*, because much of my food supply had been depleted climbing mountains and eating to keep my blood sugar level up. I was weary, took a couple of falls, but God had given me grace.

Stratton, Maine

The first trail town beyond Andover was Stratton. That would be the goal line the next day. Three mountains stretched between camp and Stratton: Crocker South and North, and Spaulding.

The white blaze was crowded as I introduced myself to twelve hikers. On mile fourteen just before crossing US 27, I walked up behind a couple and their two sons who agreed to give me a ride into town.

After checking a couple of motels, I settled in at the White Wolf Inn and enjoyed a hot shower and supper at the motel restaurant. It was mouth-watering chicken vegetable soup and salad. Plans for Sunday morning were a hearty breakfast, church, and be back on the trail by mid-morning.

This trek through the lobster state was proving the motto: "No rain, no pain, no Maine" to be correct. There was a little of both. The lay of the land could wear down the most spirited backpacker. Yet, there was something spectacular about it all, too.

Breakfast was one to remember. I joined a table of hikers in an overflowing booth in the small town grill. There I heard the stories of *Rock* (who had been on the trail for nine years), he was a teacher from Ohio, *Spoon* from New Zealand, Andy and Lorie, who were also from Ohio, and a very talkative trekker from Vermont that had done everything and been everywhere.

Tau was in town and took me to church in her friend's van, but it did not start until eleven, so she gave me a ride to the trailhead instead. What a day it was! After luscious blueberry pancakes, two eggs, and bacon, my engines were revving for a mountain climb.

It was incredibly beautiful with blue skies, a nice breeze and a view from Avery Peak that captured my heart. When I stopped to talk to *Sweet Tea* (a young man from Georgia) and took in the panorama of mountain ranges below, it was stunning. I could count a couple of hundred peaks rising above a finger lake that glistened and glimmered in the vale to the west. The view inspired this little free verse poem:

Avery Peak

It took me by surprise. Adding the miles under my boots
the trail went up to Avery Peak for a stunning 360' view.
Over two hundred mountain peaks touched blue skies.

The lake below was stretching over the vale in broken
pieces of land and green isles like a giant serpentine.
It was one of those stop-and-take-it-in moments.
Here's a place for the memory for ordinary days
when mountain climbing is not the pursuit.
It was sight to see and an experience to cherish—
walking on top of the world with the wind in my face.

This was the land of the Bigelow Mountain range. A few weary south bounders were on the trail besides the very content and take-it-easy *Sweet Tea*.

When I asked his trail name, he said it was "Swaaat Tay."

I asked him to come again and then I understood the thick southern accent. *Stray* was a young lady from Tennessee, and *Serge* was from Russia. Farther along came two brothers and one of their sons out for an overnighter. Their home was nearby in Millinocket, Maine.

The liveliest personality I saw that day was the infamous partridge with her brood of chicks. I banged my hiking poles together to scare her off. She paralleled me going up the trail. She wanted to be sure I was leaving the vicinity, so she gave me a personal escort. What a fuss she made.

The fifteen miles of high mountain elevations should have been taxing, but I was coming from a town stop, refreshed and refueled. That night I was solo in the shelter at Little Bigelow Lean-to. It was quiet, and I slept until the sun rose over the eastern horizon at 5 A.M.

The trail was smooth Monday, but the bugs were torturous, and a red-tail hawk made me feel very unwelcome. He dove at me four times until I resorted to whizzing a rock or two by his head. Apparently, I had invaded his territory. Other hikers shared the same story of his escapades that day.

Pierce Pond

As I walked that summer day, there were white bunchberries every-where. Seventeen miles and nine hours later, I pulled off the pack at Pierce

Pond. The shelter, perched on the pond, was full of people milling about, and tent sites were loaded with spirited lads.

As the custom was in the trail community, the menagerie of hikers made room for one more. *Grey Eagle* from Georgia was tent camping. Murphy, Emily and *Whiskers*, all from Florida, were in the shelter along with Garrit from Maine. Their nightspots were picked out, and food bags hung on rodent-free lines with protective tin cans attached overhead.

All of us plus a few more sat by the campfire that night as the sun went down behind the pond. There were always stories to tell, and Murphy had the upper-hand on all of us. He was a spunky and saucy middle-aged man with double prosthetics.

I watched as he broke firewood over his steel legs and fed the yellow blaze.

Four of us signed up for the twelve-pancake breakfast the next morning at Harrison's, a mile up the trail. When dawn broke, I had plenty of time to get ready before the 7 A.M. appointment. It was worth the seven dollars without a doubt—blueberry cakes, milk, tea, and meat. What a joy to pray over the daybreak meal, the request of *Grey Eagle* when he learned what I did for a living. *Boogey Man*, *Pokey*, Garrit, *Grey Eagle*, and Tim Harrison all said, "Amen."

Day seven was a nineteen-mile hike with the great jumpstart breakfast, but it was misery when it came to the battle of the bugs. I finally resorted at the end of the day to tying my long sleeve cool-max shirt to my head like a turban to get some relief.

Garrit and I walked to the Kennebec River and talked about family, faith, and evolution. It rained as we spoke. A running river was off to our right, adjacent to the up and down footpath. He said he was an atheist.

Our talk was quite a contrast to my conversation with Murphy earlier that morning. Murphy saw me reading the Bible and asked me several questions, revealing his own honest struggles with living out the faith.

The atheist and the preacher crossed the Kennebec at 9:30 A.M. in a canoe guided by *Hillbilly* from West Virginia. Kennebec had claimed the life of a backpacker years before, so the National Park Service provided the canoe crossing.

On the south side of the river, we met *Smoky* from Tennessee, and *Princess*

Brat and *Alpine* from Georgia. Garrit went into Caratunk to buy supplies, and I pressed on for sixteen more miles.

Other hikers on that day were *Fiesta* and *Siesta*, two men from Knoxville, Tennessee, and *Lunar* and *Solar*, newlyweds from Georgia.

Monson, Maine

The shelter that night was quiet and empty. The water source was very good. My thoughts turned toward the big town stop the following day. Monson was the last civilized spot on the map before the one hundred-mile wilderness. It was also home to Shaw's, the best-known hikers' hostel up and down two thousand miles of trail. They were known for their 2x2x2's or their 3x3x3's. It was breakfast with two pancakes, two eggs, two sausages, etc.

There was one hard day's hike first. I left Bald Mountain an hour after daybreak and put one step in front of the other for eleven hours covering twenty-two miles. The woodlands were full of critters and travelers. Among the wildlife were deer, a pair of owls, squirrels, and those fun-loving chipmunks.

It was a long day, and I had to check my attitude as I added up the miles and did combat with kamikaze mosquitoes. Moxie Mountain had a nice view. Mileage miscalculations placed me on a dirt road leading to Monson rather than Highway 15, where the one hundred-mile wilderness began. I had to hike 3.3 more miles than I had planned.

My boots hit the pavement at 5 P.M., where Matt, Stan, and Steve were just walking out of the one-hundred-mile wilderness after fifty miles of backpacking. Gear was scattered everywhere. Their skin was raw with bug bites. The men were university students from Massachusetts. They were more than kind, unloaded some trail food on me, and took me into town. What a relief.

When we pulled up at Shaw's, I felt like a whipped puppy but a slap-happy one. Chuck Norris from Texas was there (not the martial arts expert and actor), *Hedgehog* from Indiana, Aaron from Georgia, Emily from Ohio, and Justin from Maryland, along with *Traveler* from Amsterdam.

I took special interest in talking further with *Traveler* (a trail legend) and hearing his anecdotes.

Traveler's given name was Greg Key and he had hiked the trail eighteen times or so; this time twice, north then south. He had contracted Lyme Disease in New Jersey. As a result, doctors had strongly recommended that he not hike in the direct sunlight due to a rash that developed. At times, he would hike thirty-five to forty miles in one night and day combined. I bunked in a big room of twin beds along with *Traveler*. Late that afternoon, he sat in a rocker and filled my imagination with his years of trail lore.

The shower was better-than great. Then it was time for laundry and a re-supply run into the small business district. Monson was small town America with a friendly disposition. My feet were tender as I walked down the streets to restock on trail food at two stores. One proprietor said I smiled the whole time I was in the store. It was just good to be there with only 117 miles to go.

A chicken salad and pitcher of water served as a feast for supper. Once back at the boarding house, I called home. One of the young boys in our church had been kicked by a horse and he was hanging in the balance of life and death for a couple of days. Finding cell phone reception out in the street, I prayed with the young man's father who was at the Children's Hospital critical care wing in Knoxville, Tennessee.

Prune Picker could not make it. My old seminary friend and hiking brother would not be able to finish as we had hoped and planned. He had injured his back and there was no way he could make the miles with a thirty-pound pack.

John Jordan (*Morning Glory*) would come in the next day to join me for the one hundred-mile wilderness. He had driven up with his wife and four boys to his wife's hometown in Maine all the way from East Tennessee. He arrived at 8 A.M., just after I had the 2x2x2 famous Shaw breakfast. Rain was falling from cloudy skies.

Before we loaded up for the final trek, I spoke to my sweetheart one more time. This was day nine, and I missed her like crazy. I said farewell to *Traveler*, and he invited me to Amsterdam for a visit. He was waiting on *Tau* before he entered the one hundred-mile wilderness.

The One-Hundred Mile Wilderness

We traveled ten easy miles. John (*Glory*) even fished a little at a pond, but didn't get any nibbles. We started strong with a three-mile-per-hour pace, but then *Glory* began to feel woozy. He asked me to meet him at the shelter. Once there, I cooked a chicken noodle dinner and waited for him to come in.

A mile before camp there was a stream to ford. Maine was well-known for such crossings, often without any footbridge or rope lines. I had a little concern for *Glory* making the crossing, but he had no trouble. He just wasn't in any hurry.

Along the way that day we met six other hikers going southbound. Among them were *Far Sun* from Johnson City, Tennessee, *Grizzly* from Georgia, and two from North Carolina called *Pipes* and *Staying*. It continued to rain off and on. We took in a great view of a waterfall on the side of the trail early in the afternoon.

When *Glory* came in, we had one of those long talks until the sun's light went out behind the hardwoods of Maine's wild lands. He smoked his pipe. Though I am anti-tobacco, the smell of the pipe begs for a yarn (interesting stories and tales). We slept to the buzz of mosquitoes, not realizing this would be our last night together on the trail.

On the tenth day, *Glory* and I crossed over a series of mountaintops that overlooked rugged country that had forever been left alone by plow, road crews, and city planners.

Only survey teams had been there to chart and pinpoint places like Barren Mountain.

We were on the trail before 6 A.M. *Glory* had left a little earlier, and I soon caught up. There was a buck that morning making all kinds of racket. So much so that my partner thought it was a moose. He soon sent me on ahead.

As I climbed the steep grades crawling north, I met a solo hiker from my sweetheart's hometown of St. Augustine, Florida. Hikers representing all parts of our land and the world were taking the mountain journey. No telling where the next one would come from and what story they had to tell. The day was pleasant as I walked near flowing waterfalls and forded a stream or two.

When I came to the sign for Cloud Pond Lean-to about mid-morning, I pulled off my backpack and waited for *Glory* to catch up. He didn't show for two hours, and I was stir-crazy thinking about the many miles to go. When I did see him, he said he was finished.

His plan was to take the afternoon and night in the shelter, hike to a road the next day, and hitch back to Monson. Though I was disappointed, it was also a relief. I knew the clock was ticking, and I had less than a week to summit.

While I sat at the crossroads waiting for *Glory*, *Red* from Vermont grunted at me as he passed by the fork in the trail. He seemed a bit curious why I asked him so many questions to make conversation. Yoram and Geraldine from Germany also came along later on. They intended to make it to Cloud Pond Lean-to, where *Glory* was staying.

Making the adjustment back to being alone again, I double-clicked after having such a long lunch break and finished the sixteen-mile day at Chairback Gap. Tina Dean from Tennessee was already there, her gear unpacked. She was stoking a small fire. Tina thought I might be her friend, Scott from Maryland, who usually caught up with her at the end of the day.

Scott came in within an hour of my arrival. The sun set and the three of us talked a little. Scott was an active duty Marine. Tina worked and lived in Knoxville, Tennessee. She was a committed Christian believer. We all slept like we had worked a twelve-hour day at hard labor—and we had.

Our gear was hung up here and there. Our pads and sleeping bags were rolled out side-by-side with stoves nearby. Food bags were hung overhead, and trekking poles rested against the walls of the lean-to. This was the life of a backpacker—a tribe with grit and a love for the grandeur God alone can make.

North was down a steep bank the next morning, where the water source was a pool of black water. (Fortunately, it was the mud that was black at the bottom while the water was clear on top.) After tanking up, I entered the wood line to start the seventeen-mile trek.

It was a beautiful morning, and I had plenty of company coming south on the trail: *Gator*, a lady from Ocala, Florida, *Z-Man* who said he lived on the trail, *Curly* from New York, Josh from Indiana, Dave, a trail runner, Rebecca from Seattle, Washington, and Eric from California.

The Gulf Hagas Mountain region was bustling with hikers, including an outward-bound group of fourteen or so fixing peanut butter and jam sandwiches.

About mid-afternoon, I met *Moose Legs* (Jay from Maine), who was running some supplies to a trail crew. He had hiked the trail a few years prior and was tagged with his name due to his speed and state of origin. He loved the wilderness and it showed.

Logan Brook Lean-to was on the backside of White Cap Mountain where the trail crew worked from a tent nearby. I was alone in the shelter, but the crew invited me down later in the evening for cookies. The water source was abundant just a few feet in front of the rough-hewn, three-sided shelter, my home for the night. Mice were known to inhabit this shelter, but they didn't trouble me that night.

The trail crew was Sarah from Oregon, Christopher from Maine, Lee from England, Bryan from Minnesota, and Jay (*Moose Legs*) from Maine. Jay was out on his errand until after dark. They shared their food that night and the next morning too. Jay had a tortilla with meat and sauce set aside for me on my way down the mountain.

White House Landing

A plan to push forward began to rise in my mind as I backpacked downhill for twelve hours. I hoped to summit on July fourth, two days early. In order to do that, it would be a twenty-five-mile hike to White House Landing. This was the only re-supply post in the one hundred-mile wilderness.

On that summer day, I counted seventeen hikers from Connecticut, New York, Virginia, Pennsylvania, Missouri, Massachusetts, Florida, and Ohio. The most intriguing were two past-middle-age ladies recovering from the hard foot travel, sitting by a bridge and road crossing. The spot was surprisingly busy with vehicle traffic right in the middle of the wilderness. The ladies' names were *Laughing Socks* from Virginia and *Rambling Tanager* from Pennsylvania. We exchanged trail experiences. I shared the faith, and then bid them safe travels.

It took a little bit to figure out where White House Landing was since the park service did not allow advertisement on the trail. I had been told there was a blue blaze trail leading to the east. I took a road and doubled back at one point, then finally found an old roadbed with the blue blazes a couple of miles later.

The trail wound through wet woodlands to a dock on a lake, where a note was attached to a foghorn instructing hikers to blow once to alert the proprietors and wait. It was 6 P.M. Bill came for me in a motorboat. We crossed Pemadumcook Lake, and then walked up a lush green hill to the wilderness lodge.

It was good to get in with the prospect of a square meal and a shower. I gobbled down a half-pound burger with an orange soft drink while sitting in the small dining room. I had it all to myself. Linda, Bill's wife, was there and had cooked the tasty supper. As I ate, I eyed the supplies in a cabinet across the dining room.

I rejoiced in having a little cabin to myself. As I washed my laundry, God "painted" a rainbow over Pemadumcook Lake. As my grandmother used to do, I washed my clothes with an old washtub and scrub board. As the sun went down, I thought how she would have laughed at the job I did. It wasn't much to brag about, just good enough to get the dirt and sweat out.

The cell phone reception was good, so I called family and friends. *Glory* said he got out and went to his wife's home in Topsham, Maine. He had hiked out of the wilderness to a road and then hitchhiked a couple of times to get back to his car at Shaw's in Monson.

About nine, the foghorn sounded across the lake. A hiker was waiting out there in the dark, but no one could get him that night due to the rocks jutting out of the lake. *Trail Blazer* from Maine spent the night camping on the wooden dock inside his tent.

It was a Sunday. There was no church in many a mile, but I praised God for the grace to get to the wilderness landing where I could replenish for the final three days on the Appalachian Trail.

Morning came on the lakeside wilderness resort and there wasn't a moose in sight. Bill had said I might spot one early morning along the lakeshore—but nothing doing. The silver water shimmered below as my eye watched the red, white, and blue fly overhead on a flagpole in the middle of the camp. The day was full of promise, and I only had sixteen miles to do.

After an incredible breakfast, I boarded the motor craft for the ride back to the blue blaze trail. Bill told me there was an aluminum fishing boat built back in the fifties called the *Arkansas Traveler*. At one time he had eight of the boats there at the wilderness resort.

On day thirteen I met some notable characters: *Rambler* from Pennsylvania, *Missing Link* from Georgia, *Mojo* from Ohio, *Boone* and *Follower* from Iowa, and *Timeless* from North Carolina. There were six others who used their first names from states like New Hampshire, Rhode Island, and New York. The two Iowans were ragtag brothers who had a mean pace, covering close to thirty miles a day.

The mosquitoes were like a black cloud swarming about me. They sounded like a buzz saw in my ear. Rainbow Stream Lean-to was not what I expected. The water was a fast current out in front of the simple shelter. It was a bit warm and tasted as though it had suds in it. My only companions had six legs and a thirst for blood. I hoped they would camp elsewhere.

Late that day, John from Montana came into the shelter. He was wet and weary. I actually got his water supply for him because he was too tired to get back up and fill his water bottles. A former park service employee out west, he had hiked a twenty-five-mile day. He slept in his trail clothes that night.

When morning came, I stirred early and packed out for my own twenty-five miles to the Katahdin Stream base camp. On many long stretches, especially when I was hiking solo, my mind would run free, and I would drink deep in quiet meditation. My heart would sing and bask in the solitary hours.

Here are a few lines that celebrated such times:

Ninety Hours of Thinking

The world gets sorted out quickly.
Prayers roll from a grateful heart.
There is a purifying effect to it all,
more grace for life and more patience.
A fresh determination works down deep
beneath the physical beating you take.
Life is reduced down to simple survival
and needing a reliable water source.
Whatever is out of sync lines up so you
can move like the wind at His command.
You learn the perfect pitch of the morning,
for your heart sings heavenly tunes.

Music in the Forest

Water rumbles from below in laughing brooks
while birds sing from above for all their worth.
There's music in the forest glades and the rustle
from the leaves is high up in majestic trees.
It is a sweet sound to hear the voice of a man
after days and hours without any conversation.
There's the rumble of the road in the distance
and the stillness of hearing your own footfalls.
In the forest are sights and sure discoveries,
and there's sound, at times wrapped in mystery.
You hear your own thoughts, and the rhythm
in the woods puts your heart back in tune.

It would be the last day I would get to experience the Appalachian Trail before coming into the well-traveled Baxter State Park (BSP). Along the way, I was introduced to David and Thomas from Oregon, *Craven* and *Woody* from Texas, and nine young ladies from all over New England going for seven weeks from Katahdin to Gorham, New Hampshire.

Then there was Gerald, a frustrated prosecuting attorney from Atlanta, Georgia. He was in the deep woods unloading his mind and thinking about life beyond politics. Later, I met *Tea Leaf* from Rochester, New York, Nathan and Betsy from Richmond, Virginia, and Brian who was also from Rochester, New York.

Baxter State Park

Once I crossed the state park boundary and came to the Abol Bridge, I had a barbecue sandwich and apple juice for a late lunch. Chad, who was from Texas, was going southbound, as were Brad and Julie from Ohio, and then there was Steve Holmes from Mechanic Falls, Maine.

The bugs kept biting and I kept hiking. That night I was solo in the shelters called the Birches, reserved for north bounders. Paul Corrigan, the Baxter State Park ranger, was a great help in preparing me for the big mountain the following day.

Could it be that it all came down to this? Day 149 was going to break tomorrow on July 4th, when I would stand on top of the American landmark.

All the years and miles had finally given way to these last few lengths up to the tableland of Maine. God had given grace when I was weary and past my limit at times, stumbling from mile marker to mile marker. I looked forward to finishing and returning to simple town pleasures, yet I would miss the smell of the forest and the rapture of the ridgelines.

My daughter, now eighteen, had written a note that I had packed along with prayer requests from my people in the church back home in Tennessee. Here's how it read:

> *Dad—*
> *Well, you are finally getting to finish the*
> *A.T. Can you believe you are in the last couple*
> *hundred miles of this incredibly long trail? I*
> *hope that you will thoroughly enjoy your time*
> *in the wilderness, so you can clear your*
> *head...Anyway I just wanted to give you a little*
> *money so you can grab a candy bar or*
> *something. I'll be thinking about you and*
> *praying for your safety...towards the end of*
> *the trail. Much love—Karis.*

It was still dark when I arose for the last day in a long journey. The Appalachian Trail was a dream when I was eighteen, and now it was a reality at age forty-eight. The Appalachian Trail Conservancy says it is a journey of five million steps, and I had estimated it cost me as a section-hiker no less than $10,870 to get it done, about five dollars a mile.

There was only one name on the trail registry before I wrote mine. I met two other hikers on the climb up, and once on the summit, there were seven day-hikers taking in the top of the world for Maine.

It was a climb of 5.2 miles to Katahdin's peak. The first mile was gentle, the second a little harder, and by the third and fourth miles you were scrambling over giant boulders with iron rungs. Then you picked your way up what I called "the dragon's spine." That is what it looked like from below. The last mile was on top before a little rise to the summit.

The climb took 3 1/2 hours up and 3 1/2 hours back in addition to 1 1/2 hours on top talking to day hikers from Maine. One of the gentlemen had climbed Katahdin's summit some fifty-three times and had never met anyone who had finished the entire walk from Georgia.

We all snacked and snapped pictures of the worn wooden marker weathered by time with thousands of hand grips and a few hundred etchings.

When you reach a place in time and eternity like that, you've got to grab hold of the goal. You've got to touch it to know it's real. I didn't cry or shout. There was no big emotional rush. I was just glad to be there and to look forward to other life goals. After bidding farewell to Brook, Rich and Cheryl, Cal and Janet, I walked south.

There's the Arkansas Traveler at the end of a thirty-year dream.

As I descended, there were ten hikers coming up (including Steve Holmes, whom I had met the day before). Also, of note were Opie and his parents: Opie and Darlene. The son was climbing Katahdin to start his southbound hike back to his home state of Georgie. His first day on the trail was my last day.

There was no water source on top, and my lips were unusually parched, so on the way down, once I got past the dragon's spine, I did a blood sugar check. It was high, so I took a shot of insulin. Water was abundant the last three miles, and I drank deeply.

The last mile before Katahdin Stream campground, I met a father with his two sons. They were taking a stroll to the Katahdin Springs waterfall. They sure put me in mind of my boys hiking the first fifty miles of the trail. This Dad was only going for a few miles with his sons—smart Dad.

When I returned the daypack back at the ranger station (I had left my much larger backpack there), I arranged for one more night's stay. I was alone in the camp where I feasted on teriyaki noodles while the mosquitoes feasted on me. I could sleep in the next morning. *Glory* would meet me at the road in front of the campground around 10 A.M.

It was the fourth of July, but there were no fireworks, just a quiet celebration after climbing what the Abenaki Indians called Katahdin, "the greatest mountain." Hallelujah. It's done.

One of my keepsakes from the Appalachian Trail is a piece of granite from Katahdin. A short poem tells the story:

The Katahdin Rock

Pursue your dreams.
No matter how long.
No matter how hard.
No matter how high.
Come to the image of God.

All our dreams and pursuits should shape us in the image of God. All of life will reveal that He stood in the shadows. He guided our footfalls. He kept us safe. He was there. If only we knew.

Now in this final chapter, words from the heights of Katahdin and a few sacred truths I learned along the way:

Katahdin's Lofty Height

As the morning sun blinds my eyes, I climb
the last mountain on the Appalachian Trail.
It is a boulder climb fitting for the end.
Something like ascending a dragon's spine,
I edge closer on final steps of two thousand miles,
fourteen-year journey from Georgia to Maine.

Water is abundant on the trail before
the boulder climb reaches for true north.
But once on top of the ridge walk, it is dry.
Flowers poke through the rocky terrain
in a field full of pink and white granite.
This is Katahdin, the dream mountain.

Giving a little blood, swatting a few flies,
I am heading for the heights where all Maine
lies beneath in lakes and rolling woodlands.
It is a rugged land tempered by hard seasons.
Other mountain peaks stand tall under blue skies,
invaded by patches of white and gray cloud cover.

Just as I reach the sign marking that final spot, another hiker greets me from a trail on my left. A group of five day-hikers rally at the top. Later a young man and a couple or two join us on the summit of this renowned mountain peak. They're all from Maine while I hail from the south. It's done. No tears, no shouts, just quiet congrats and the joy of reaching this pinnacle in life. There's also a deep recognition of the grace of God that got me from my southern homeland to this northern woodlands and the peaks beneath my feet. I stand humble on Katahdin's lofty height and smile.

Ten Sacred Truths

1. You must go down a few steps before you ever reach the goal upon the heights—that is just how real mountains are made.

2. You have to contend with bugs, boulders, and blisters to get vistas, victory, and virtue in the real world.

3. Big goals require pain, tenacity, and prayer.

4. People's stories make climbing mountains worth it all as you meet up with such intriguing personalities along the way.

5. When you are dead tired and there is no more petrol in your engine—take another step anyway.

6. Never underestimate a little encouragement and the strength of the cheering attitude.

7. Get use to the mud, rocks, and roots—they are the ever-present obstacles along the way, just keep going for the better paths ahead.

8. Find the little joys along the steep and rocky way or you'll fall beneath the gloom of those ten-to-twelve-hour days.

9. Hear the voice of God in the mountain breeze, listen to the caution of the Spirit's promptings, and have the attitude of the Nazarene carpenter in all things.

10. Work hard for worthy goals, drink deep of each
    day's pleasures, and rest well while your feet
    heal for another day in the woods.

For, lo, he that formeth the mountains, and createth the wind, and declareth unto man what is his thought, who maketh the morning darkness, and treadeth upon the high places of the earth, the Lord, the God of hosts, is his name.   (Amos 4:13)

EPILOGUE:
FAITH AND ADVENTURE

As close as I can count, there are some 237 mountain climbs on the Appalachian Trail. It is estimated that three to four million people hike a section of the trail each year. Since 1936, some 20,345 (2018 figure) have completed the entire trail. The 10,000th person to finish the trail happened in 2008. The Appalachian Trail Conservancy calls these trekkers "2,000 milers."

Available statistics reveal that in 2018 there were 4,399 backpackers who started the long journey and 19% finished who were going northbound and 26% finished who went southbound.

Eighty-five percent began at Springer Mountain like I did. Ten percent started at Katahdin. Three percent flip-flopped (hiking the entire trail on an alternate itinerary).

One way to view the dropout rate is to follow the number of northbounders who reported in 2018 at the following mile makers: 3,862 started from Springer, 1,643 made it to Harpers Ferry, 728 completed it at Katahdin. While 420 started from Katahdin, 381 made it to Kennebec Ferry, 226 to Harpers Ferry, and 111 to Springer.

As for section-hikers, twenty-five percent finished (2008). Most section-hikers cover multiple years as I did. Though they are a minority on the trail, as the years passed by I met more and more section-hikers who intended to finish every mile. Some were taking as long as thirty years to reach their goal.

The oldest recorded thru-hiker was Lee Barry, age eighty-one, who hiked the Appalachian Trail five times. How about the unnamed gentleman who took four years to section hike the entire trail, finishing at the age of eighty-six? The youngest that completed the trail was a six-year-old boy. Another six-year-old finished with his eight-year-old sister.

One three-year-old young lady started a section hike and finished when she was fifteen. On the other side of the spectrum, a sixty-nine year old lady did a section-hike and completed it when she was eighty. In fact, ladies make up twenty-five percent of those who complete the entire trail. One lady hiked the trail three times at ages sixty-seven, sixty-nine, seventy-six. More recent statistics say that 1/3 of backpackers are now women.

Then there are those like Traveler from Amsterdam who have hiked the trail over and over again. Some 125 have hiked the Appalachian Trail two or more times, and thirty have finished it three or more times. Once is enough for me. (The fact is—I owe fourteen years of vacation time to my family. That is, their kind of vacation time—not mine.)

These hardy backpackers come from every state in the union and a growing list of international countries:

Australia	Israel
Austria	Japan
Bahamas	Mexico
Belgium	Morocco
Canada	New Zealand
Chile	Norway
Czech Republic	Philippines
Denmark	Scotland
England	Singapore
Finland	South Africa
France	Spain
Germany	Sweden
Holland	Switzerland
India	Wales
Ireland	

As I traveled the trail year by year, I met very few backpackers from my native state, though there were a lot from Tennessee, where my wife and I served in ministry for those years and raised our family.

If you ever consider a crazy project like hiking the Appalachian Trail, there is the promise of a multiple of extraordinary challenges. Yet, along the way there are stories you will hear and tales you will become part of yourself.

There is no doubt in my mind that God walks in those mountains, and He will take you on many adventures if you'll hear His voice and see His hand.

The Almighty has been with me in many places around the world. It is good to know He's there. I'll never forget that He walked with me along the Appalachian Trail. There we traveled five million steps. Once, I thought it was the call of the wild that I loved. I have since discovered it was His voice that spoke to me there.

Finding True North

All of us have been lost at one point or the other. GPS (Global Positioning System) and maps help. But in life how do you find true north? All philosophies, worldviews and religious perspectives come to a dead end except for the Christian faith where there is hope and answers to the hard questions.

There is no doubt that many who call themselves Christians are not, but there are those who honor the Gospel and align their lives by the New Testament to point north, and such faith does not disappoint.

1. God created the heavens and the earth, just as the Bible says, in six literal days. We have just over 6,000 years of recorded human history. False science does not change that. True science proves a young earth and belief in the Creator. What we see in creation is not happenstance (www.answersingenesis.com and www.icr.org).

2. Not only is there a Creator, there is a Redeemer, and His name is Jesus Christ. He is not a cuss word or a reference to blasphemy. He is God in the flesh with the mission to redeem sinful men. All of us are sinful and all of us need the Savior. There is none other. He is able to save us because He is God.

3. There is no doubt that we are not blank slates. All of us are tainted with sin in thought, word and deed. There is evil (the rejection of God) in the world and there is evil in all of us to one degree or the other. The rejection of God produces arrogance and ignorance so that we become fools. True wisdom is only found in God.

4. Without bowing the knee to God and seeing Him
   as Creator and Redeemer, we become immoral,
   unethical and relativists disbelieving in absolutes—
   except that there are no absolutes. But there are
   rights and wrongs, absolutes, and a moral
   compass. They are the Ten Commandments. All
   men have some form of an innate moral code.

5. None of us can keep the Ten Commandments
   except by the grace that is found in Jesus Christ.
   He was the son of Abraham, of the lineage of
   David, a Hebrew who loved Israel—and the Gentile
   nations. He is True North. He died for our sins
   and then broke the power of death. In Jesus is
   hope, life's answers, soul satisfaction and joy.

Finding True North is not a matter of becoming religious. The world is full of people trying to reach God through idolatry, rituals, jihad, depravation, meditation and dead works. God has reached down to us because we cannot reach up to Him. In Jesus there is forgiveness that can transform the nature of man.

There is victory over sin and its choke hold on us. He takes us through the straight gate and on the narrow path that leads to the highlands. It is a climb worth taking with unbelievable views. It is a journey to much better places than the Appalachian Trail.

How beautiful upon the mountains are the feet of him that bringeth good tidings, that publisheth peace; that bringeth good tidings of good, that publisheth salvation; that saith unto Zion, thy God reigneth. (Isaiah 52:7)

GLOSSARY

Amphibian shoes—footwear that hikers use to cross waterways. They dry out quickly and can serve as a backup for boots when they die, as mine did.

Appalachian Trail Conservancy (ATC)—once called Appalachian Trail Conference. The ATC maintains and manages the 2,176 miles (this figure is apt to change due to constant re-routing) along the Appalachian Trail that stretches from Georgia to Maine. The headquarters is located close to the halfway mark in Harpers Ferry, West Virginia.

Blow down—uprooted trees blown down by high winds.

Blue blazer—a hiker who takes a variety of side trails, often on a more scenic route, which cut short the white blaze trail, the official mark of the Appalachian Trail.

Bunchberries—dwarf dogwood bushes with dense berries.

Cabela's—outfitters store originally based in Sydney, Nebraska, now found nationwide.

Cades Cove—an eleven mile road that winds through a series of farms and passes by three churches and a national park headquarters in some of the most beautiful valley pasture land in East Tennessee, found in the Great Smoky Mountains just outside of Townsend, Tennessee.

Cairns—stacks of stones that marked the trail, especially for winter conditions when the snow covered the footpath.

Clementine—a tangerine-like fruit.

Clingman's Dome—the highest elevation on the Appalachian trail at 6,343 feet, located in the Great Smoky Mountains of East Tennessee

CoolMax—a clothing line that wicks out the sweat and keeps the body dry.

Coup—a practice of the American Plains Indians where they would swoop down riding a horse or on foot and tag the enemy or opponent to display bravery. (That is what the mosquitoes did to me time and time again.)

Damascus—biggest trail town from Georgia to Maine, located in southern Virginia at the 457-mile marker from Springer and the 1,719-mile marker from Katahdin. Many return every year for Trail Days in May for Appalachian Trail hikers' reunions.

Eft—a salamander

Flip-flopper—a hiker who takes on the trail from one end or the other, treks to the middle, flips or flops to the other end and hikes to the middle again.

Giardia—a water-borne bacterium that can disable hikers and send them for an extended stay in the hospital.

GORP—"good ole raisins and peanuts," a trail mix often combined with M&M's and yogurt bites.

Great Smoky Mountains National Park—premier park of the United States National Park system, at least in number of visitors each year. There were 8 million every year back in 2008. The 2018 figure was 11.3 million. The Appalachian Trail cuts across the park for 72 miles. The north side of the trail is Tennessee while the south side is North Carolina. Shelters are often full and running over.

Green Mountains—primary mountain range in Vermont where the Appalachian Trail and the Long Trail run together for 105 miles.

Hostel—a place to stay for hikers to get a shower, do laundry, get a ride into town to restock, and get out of the woods for a night for a few more comforts, priced at a more affordable rate than motels.

Hut—the Appalachian Mountain Club lodges found in the New Hampshire White Mountains. They have bunks, private rooms, bathrooms (but no showers), kitchens, dining halls, and fantastic views for a price. There are eight huts in all, stationed across the White Mountains.

Juncos—a dark eyed, slate-colored finch, sometimes called snow-birds.

Katahdin—the northern terminus where most Appalachian Trail hikers end their journey, others begin there. The famed mountain is located in Maine as the feature of Baxter State Park, standing at 5,269 feet.

Lean-to—Maine's version of trail shelters found in other states. These are three-sided log structures under a roof with one side exposed to the open air. They typically sleep six to eight people.

Lyme Disease—a tick-borne disease that can affect hikers with such severity it can debilitate the nervous system and put the hiker in bed back home.

Moleskin—a must for every backpacker's first aid kit. This sticky bandage provides an extra layer of skin for blistered feet.

Mount Washington—the big mountain of the Presidential range in the White Mountains of New Hampshire. Winds have been recorded at 231 mph, the record for North America. The mountain stands at 6,288 feet.

New Age Philosophy—a combination of metaphysics, theology, nature and philosophy, which centers on religious tolerance and moral diversity. It translates into doing whatever feels good as long as no one else is being hurt in the process.

North-bounder—a trekker who hikes the Appalachian Trail from Springer Mountain in Georgia to Mount Katahdin in Maine.

Paganism—has been defined as any belief outside the monotheistic faiths (belief in one God), including spiritualism (belief in contacting the spirits of the dead) and animism (belief that spirits are in all things from animals, plants, and even rocks).

Paradiddle—a little mythical red Virginia squirrel with the energy and size of a chipmunk, just a little bigger, and with a lot more mischief—if that is possible.

Pine Marten—a weasel-like mammal found in the northeast United States.

Section-hiker—a backpacker who hikes the entire trail in big or small sections over several years.

Shelter—a three-sided log or stone structure with roof, constructed along the trail every seven miles or so from Georgia to New Hampshire. At times, shelters are more elaborate with a loft and/or a fourth side.

Shenandoah National Park—named after the principle mountain range in northern Virginia. The Appalachian Trail cuts through the park for 107 miles. There is a lot of deadwood from acid rain and/or infestation. Watch out for the skunks!

Shuttle service—a list of local drivers who provide a ride to a trailhead and/or road crossing for a fee.

Slack-packer—a hiker who takes on a section trail with only a day pack or fanny pack for speed and agility, when he/she has assistance to access the trail.

Solo—a hiker who takes on the trail alone or camps alone.

South-bounder—a backpacker who hikes the trail from Mount Katahdin in Maine to Springer Mountain in Georgia.

Springer Mountain—the southern terminus where most Appalachian Trail hikers start. For others, it is the finish line. The mountain is located in Georgia as part of the Amicalola Falls State Park, standing at 3,782 feet.

Thru-hiker—a trekker who hikes the Appalachian Trail from the beginning (whether from the north or south terminus) to the finish in a single year or sequence of seasons.

Trail angel—a person who assists hikers with rides, foodstuffs, or any other kind of assistance that brings relief, joy and refreshment.

Trailhead—place where the trail crosses a road and where parking is often provided. This is a good place for section-hikers to stop and start again the next time.

Trail journal log book—a notebook found in most shelters and lean-to's in which backpackers write, date, and sign their names.

Trail magic—when good things happen that provide encouragement on a hard day or in a tight spot, when a need is met in extraordinary ways, and you get where you are going with a little grace and assistance.

Trail runners—taking on the Appalachian Trail in tennis shoes, or cross-trainers at a jog or a run, packing light and moving fast.

USFS—United States Forest Service, often the prefix marking a road in a national park region. These roads can be rough, steep, and not always well maintained.

White-blazer—a backpacker who does the trail mile-by-mile all the way as it is marked by the white rectangle from Georgia to Maine or vice versa.

White Mountains—the principle mountain range in New Hampshire.

Yellow-blazer—a hiker who walks the trail by hitting a road access, then hitting the trail, on and off again, without doing the entire footpath mile for mile.

Zen Buddhism—the belief that enlightenment can be attained through meditation, self-contemplation, and intuition rather than through faith and devotion. Zen is a Japanese word meaning "to mediate."

Zero-day—a day when the backpacker added no miles to the total in reaching the overall goal.

About the Author

Author Lon Chenowith grew up in Little Rock, Arkansas, the state where his family has lived for five generations. He has served as a pastor in Florida, West Virginia, Tennessee and North Carolina.

He is the Director of Missions for Sandy Run Baptist Association in Bostic, North Carolina, and the Director of Way of Grace International, a mission organization that evangelizes and equips Christian leaders.

When he is not hiking, he enjoys running, mountain biking and international mission work. He and his wife Kay have two sons and a daughter, four grandsons and a granddaughter.